BACKPACK BOOKS

1,001 FACTS ABOUT
SHARKS

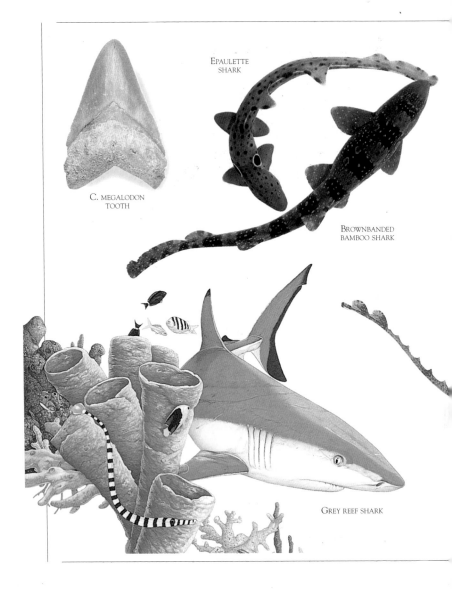

EPAULETTE
SHARK

C. MEGALODON
TOOTH

BROWNBANDED
BAMBOO SHARK

GREY REEF SHARK

BACKPACK BOOKS

1,001 FACTS ABOUT SHARKS

Written by
JOYCE POPE
Additional material
by Brian
Hunter Smart

THRESHER
SHARK

RAY

HAMMERHEAD
SHARK

DORLING KINDERSLEY
London • New York • Stuttgart • Moscow • Sydney

LONDON, NEW YORK, MUNICH
MELBOURNE, DELHI

Editor Simon Mugford
Designer Dan Green
Senior editor Andrew Macintyre
Design manager Jane Thomas
DTP designer Jill Bunyan
Production Nicola Torode
With thanks to the original team
Project editor Anna McMurray
Art editor Martin Wilson, Jacqui Burton
Senior editor Alistair Dougall
Senior art editor Carole Oliver, Sarah Crouch
Picture research Nail Aldridge
Production Kate Oliver

First published in Great Britain in 2002
by Dorling Kindersley Limited
80 Strand, London WC2R 0RL
A Penguin company

A CIP catalogue record for this book is available from
the British Library

ISBN 0 7513 4418 4

Colour reproduction by Colourscan
Printed and bound in Singapore

See our complete catalogue at
www.dk.com

CONTENTS

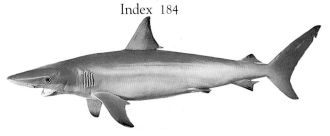

INTRODUCTION

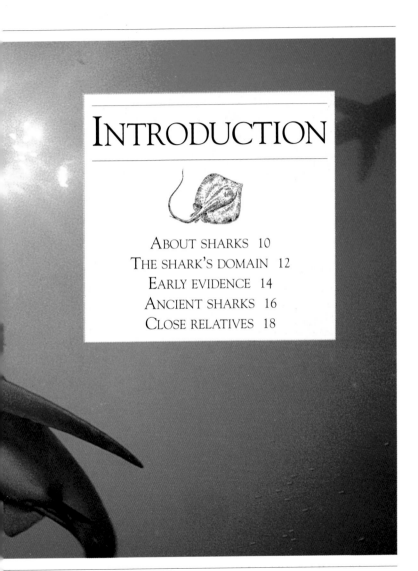

ABOUT SHARKS

SHARKS ROAM all the oceans of the world. Most are large, and all are flesh-eaters. Your first sight may be a dark, triangular fin moving steadily through the water. Closer to, you will see the series of gill slits behind the head and the pointed snout that overhangs the mouth.

HAMMERHEAD
Sharks are generally solitary creatures, but sharks such as green dogfish, blue sharks, and some kinds of hammerhead shark swim in groups.

The great white is the only shark able to lift its head out of the water to inspect surface objects

Pointed snout

Light-coloured underbelly

GREAT WHITE
There are more than 340 species of sharks. The most feared is the great white or white pointer, which lives near the surface of tropical seas. Its main food is large fish, turtles, and seals. It is big enough to regard human beings as prey and it has been responsible for many attacks on people.

Pectoral fin

ONE-YEAR-OLD LEOPARD SHARK

This shark is 38 cm (15 in) in length

SHARK SPOTS

The leopard shark gets its name from its spotted skin. Its teeth have rounded tops for crushing the hard-shelled creatures, such as clams and sea snails, on which it feeds. This shark is frequently kept in marine aquariums as it adapts well to captivity.

HORN SHARK

The horn shark is a slow, bottom-living species. It feeds on hard-shelled prey and is harmless unless disturbed. It lays eggs in spiral-shaped egg cases, which it wedges into crevices in rocks to keep them safe from enemies until they hatch.

Spotted pattern on skin

Pelvic fin

SHARK EATS MUM ALIVE AS KIDS WATCH

Horror on dive at nature spot

A MOTHER of five was bitten in two by a 13ft shark while her children watched in horror from a boat.

NEWS SENSATION

A human stands little chance in an encounter with a large shark, as this attack in Australia demonstrates. Shark attacks always make the headlines. They often take place close to land in shallow water, where children play and most people swim.

11

THE SHARK'S DOMAIN

THE WORLD'S OCEANS are the shark's domain. A few species, such as the blue shark, are found throughout the warmer parts of this vast area, but many are restricted to certain coasts or to types of watery habitat, such as muddy bays or the edges of coral reefs. The majority live in the well-lit surface zone, but a few are only found in very deep water.

SEA HOME

Nurse sharks are often found where the sea is shallow. On the outer side of a reef, where the water is deeper, species such as the blacktip reef shark abound. The blue shark and the great white, both fast-swimming hunters, and the slow-moving, huge whale shark are most often seen in the open seas. The strange-looking lantern and goblin shark live in the depths of the ocean.

Continental shelf

Continental slope

Blacktip reef shark

FRESHWATER EXPLORERS
As well as the sea, bull sharks inhabit tropical rivers and lakes. They have been spotted 3,700 km (2,298 miles) from the sea in the River Amazon. They are a great danger to other river dwellers.

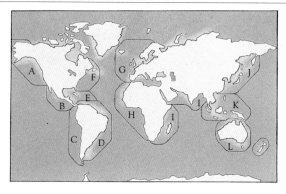

WORLD MAP

This map shows the distribution of coastal-living sharks. Some, such as the whale shark, may live in many places while the green dogfish is known from only one area. Some oceanic sharks may venture into inshore waters but do not stay there long.

A. WESTERN NORTH AMERICA: Horn shark
B. WESTERN CENTRAL AMERICA: Bull shark
C. WESTERN SOUTH AMERICA: Swell shark
D. EASTERN SOUTH AMERICA: Cookiecutter shark
E. WEST INDIES: Green dogfish
F. EASTERN NORTH AMERICA: Greenland shark

G. WESTERN EUROPE: Porbeagle
H. WEST AFRICA: Gulper shark
I. E. AFRICA, S. ASIA: Blacktip reef shark
J. NORTHEASTERN ASIA: Goblin shark
K. POLYNESIA: Whale shark
L. AUSTRALIA: Wobbegong

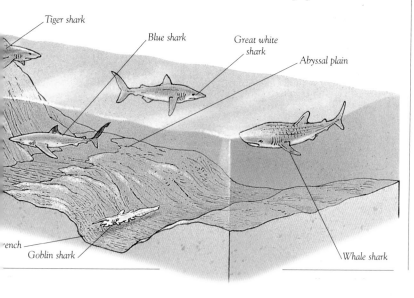

Tiger shark

Blue shark

Great white shark

Abyssal plain

ench

Goblin shark

Whale shark

EARLY EVIDENCE

THE TEETH of sharks are common fossils. The first sharks lived about 380 million years ago, in a sea that covered what is now Ohio, US. When they died, they sunk so quickly into the silt on the seabed, that their skeletons are well preserved.

SPIRAL FOSSIL TEETH
Unlike other sharks, *Helicoprion* retained its teeth in its upper and lower jaws, rather than shedding them at regular intervals. The oldest teeth are in the middle of the spiral.

Diameter of teeth whorl is about 17 cm (6.5 in)

Teeth were constantly pushed back, forming a spiral

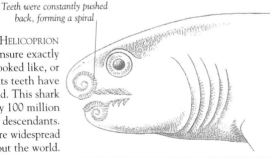

HELICOPRION
Scientists are unsure exactly what *Helicoprion* looked like, or fed on, as only its teeth have ever been found. This shark survived for nearly 100 million years but left no descendants. Its fossils are widespread throughout the world.

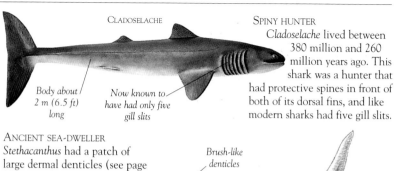

CLADOSELACHE

Body about 2 m (6.5 ft) long

Now known to have had only five gill slits

SPINY HUNTER
Cladoselache lived between 380 million and 260 million years ago. This shark was a hunter that had protective spines in front of both of its dorsal fins, and like modern sharks had five gill slits.

ANCIENT SEA-DWELLER
Stethacanthus had a patch of large dermal denticles (see page 36) on its head and on its first dorsal fin. They may have been for protection, or enabled it to latch on to bigger fish, just as the modern remora does.

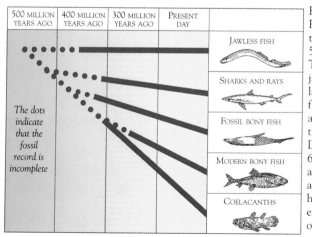

Brush-like denticles

Anal fin

Clasper

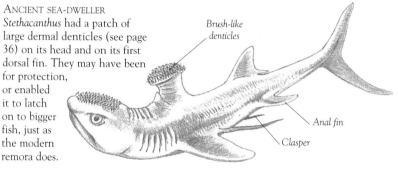

500 MILLION YEARS AGO	400 MILLION YEARS AGO	300 MILLION YEARS AGO	PRESENT DAY	
				JAWLESS FISH
				SHARKS AND RAYS
The dots indicate that the fossil record is incomplete				FOSSIL BONY FISH
				MODERN BONY FISH
				COELACANTHS

FISH EVOLUTION
Fish have lived in the sea for nearly 500 million years. The first fish were jawless, like lampreys. Modern fish appeared at the end of the Age of Dionosaurs, about 65 million years ago. *Coelacanth* and sturgeons have survived the extinction of most of their relatives.

ANCIENT SHARKS

SINCE THE FIRST SHARKS evolved, ways of
life in the sea have changed very little.
As a result, many of today's sharks are
much like their ancient ancestors –
some are so similar that
people think of them as
living fossils. As such they
can tell us a great deal about
animals that may
have been extinct
for many millions
of years.

PORT JACKSON
SHARK

OLD RELATIVES
Fossils of fish
very similar to
the Port Jackson
shark have been found in rocks 150 million
years old. They fed on hard-shelled prey such as
oysters and clams, which they crushed with
strangely shaped, ridged teeth.

ELUSIVE
SPECIES
The frilled
shark lives in
deeper water than many other
species and remained unknown
to science until the late 19th
century. Unusual-looking on
the outside, it is even
stranger under the skin, for some
parts of its skeleton resemble those of sharks
that became extinct 350 million years ago.

FRILLED
SHARK

Eel-shaped
body

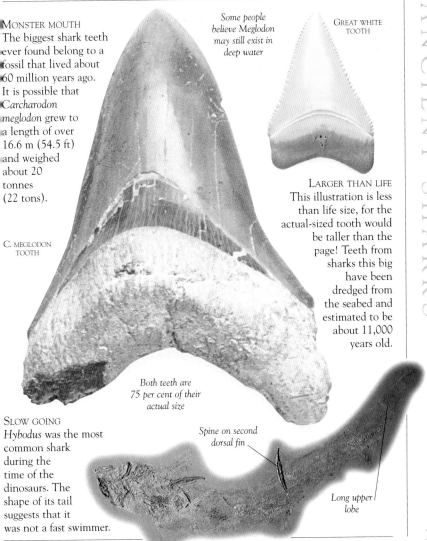

MONSTER MOUTH
The biggest shark teeth ever found belong to a fossil that lived about 60 million years ago. It is possible that *Carcharodon meglodon* grew to a length of over 16.6 m (54.5 ft) and weighed about 20 tonnes (22 tons).

Some people believe Meglodon may still exist in deep water

GREAT WHITE TOOTH

C. MEGLODON TOOTH

LARGER THAN LIFE
This illustration is less than life size, for the actual-sized tooth would be taller than the page! Teeth from sharks this big have been dredged from the seabed and estimated to be about 11,000 years old.

Both teeth are 75 per cent of their actual size

SLOW GOING
Hybodus was the most common shark during the time of the dinosaurs. The shape of its tail suggests that it was not a fast swimmer.

Spine on second dorsal fin

Long upper lobe

17

CLOSE RELATIVES

IT IS HARD TO BELIEVE that flat, slow-moving skates and rays, which live on the bed of the sea, are related to fast, streamlined sharks. However, rays' and sharks' anatomy is very similar: for example, both have cartilaginous skeletons (see page 34) and up to seven gill slits.

Underside is pale in colour, while upper surface is camouflaged

SEABED FEEDER
Rays feed mainly on sand-living creatures, so their mouths are on the underside of their bodies. There is a hole called a spiracle on the upper side, through which clean water for breathing is taken in and passed over the gills.

MOLLUSCS
Rays feed on hard-shelled animals, such as sea snails, that live in the sand.

Grinding teeth crush the armour of prey

POISON GLAND
Some rays have sharp, saw-like stings on their tails. These are good protection against their enemies.

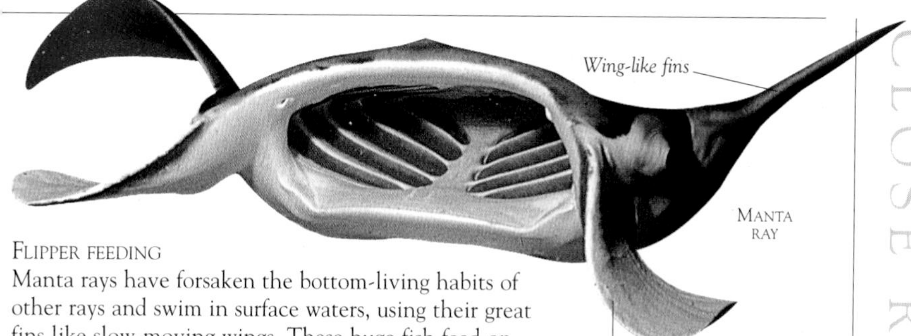

Wing-like fins

MANTA
RAY

FLIPPER FEEDING
Manta rays have forsaken the bottom-living habits of
other rays and swim in surface waters, using their great
fins like slow-moving wings. These huge fish feed on
plankton, which they guide into their mouths with
flipper-like organs on either side of their heads.

Flippers for
guiding food

SUN BATHER
The pygmy devil ray is smaller than
the great manta. In warm seas, it can
sometimes be seen lying on the surface,
before leaping out of the water
and speeding away.

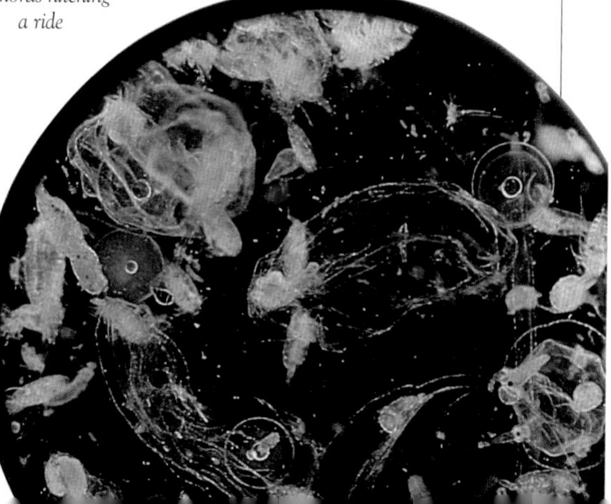

MOBULA
WITH
REMORAS

Remoras hitching
a ride

FLOATING FOOD
Plankton is largely made up
of tiny marine plants and
animals that float at the
mercy of the currents.
This nutritious "soup"
drifts on or near the
surface of the sea.

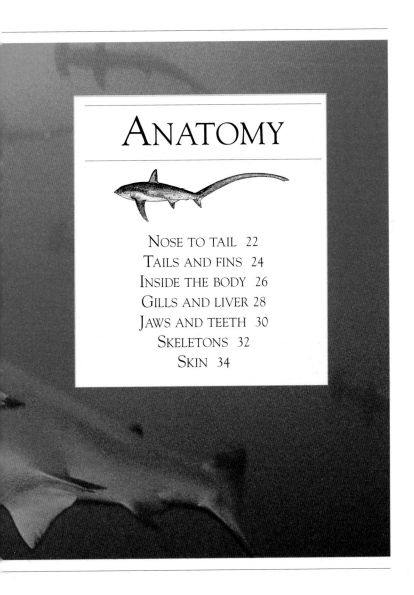

ANATOMY

NOSE TO TAIL

MOST SHARKS are large fish, designed for constant, effortless swimming, though not at sustained high speeds. Their colour is usually a blueish-grey, to blend with the colours of the ocean. Their senses, like their teeth, are razor-sharp, and they are quick to investigate anything that could be food.

Long gill slits

Near symmetrical long upper and lower caudal (tail) lobes

Swimming keel

Pelvic fin

HARMLESS FISH
The largest fish in the world is the whale shark which can reach 13 m (43 ft) long and weigh 22 tonnes (24 tons). Like the largest of the whales, these fish feed on very small organisms that they strain from the sea.

This drawing of a person to scale gives an idea of the whale shark's large size

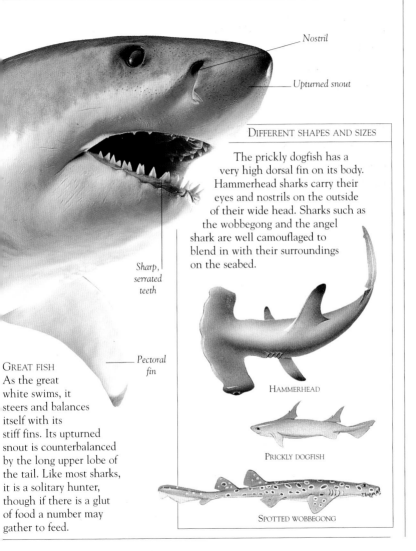

Nostril

Upturned snout

DIFFERENT SHAPES AND SIZES

The prickly dogfish has a very high dorsal fin on its body. Hammerhead sharks carry their eyes and nostrils on the outside of their wide head. Sharks such as the wobbegong and the angel shark are well camouflaged to blend in with their surroundings on the seabed.

Sharp, serrated teeth

HAMMERHEAD

PRICKLY DOGFISH

SPOTTED WOBBEGONG

Pectoral fin

GREAT FISH
As the great white swims, it steers and balances itself with its stiff fins. Its upturned snout is counterbalanced by the long upper lobe of the tail. Like most sharks, it is a solitary hunter, though if there is a glut of food a number may gather to feed.

23

TAILS & FINS

A SHARK PROPELS itself through the water by moving its powerful tail from side to side. Unlike most fish, a shark's fins are supported internally by rods of cartilage. They cannot be folded against its body but project outwards, controlling the direction of the shark and acting as a braking mechanism.

SWIMMING AID
The shape of a shark's tail is important to the speed it can swim. Sharks with evenly balanced caudal fins (tails) are the fastest swimmers, whereas slower sharks may have hardly any lower lobe to their tail.

THRASHING TAIL
A thresher shark uses its tail to help it get food. Beating the water with the long upper lobe of its tail frightens and stuns small fish, making them easier to catch.

Enlarged upper caudal lobe

FAST-MOVING
Each stroke of the tail tends to drive the great white downward, since the upper lobe is slightly longer. However, water movement round the upturned snout keeps the shark balanced.

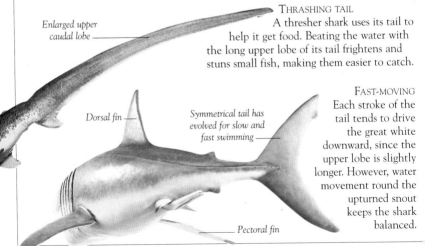

Dorsal fin

Symmetrical tail has evolved for slow and fast swimming

Pectoral fin

UNIQUE TAIL
Angel sharks have very large fins, which make them look like skates. Like skates, they live on the seabed, but they swim like sharks, using their slender tails and not their fins for propulsion. Unlike most sharks, the lower lobe of an angel shark's tail is bigger than the upper lobe.

SHAPELY TAIL
The swell shark, which lives in kelp beds close to the shore, has a tail that is not designed for fast swimming. In spite of this, the swell shark is a very effective hunter of small fish.

Anal fin

TAIL OF SWELL SHARK

SEABED DWELLER
The horn shark has large fins and a small tail for its size. Tagging has shown that it sometimes swims long distances from its breeding areas.

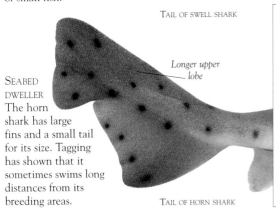

Longer upper lobe

TAIL OF HORN SHARK

FIN FACTS

• Sharks steer using their paired (pectoral and pelvic) fins which function like the wings of an aircraft.

• The horny rods of shark fins are cut off and dried to make soup.

• The inner edge of the male's pelvic fins forms a pair of mating organs called claspers.

25

INSIDE THE BODY

IMMEDIATELY BENEATH the skin of a shark lie the zigzag muscles that swing the body from side to side as it swims. In the body cavity below is the heart and digestive system. The intestine is fairly straight, apart from the spiral valve, which adds to the area in which digested food can be absorbed. Contrary to popular belief, sharks are not stupid animals and have a larger brain for their body size than most bony fish.

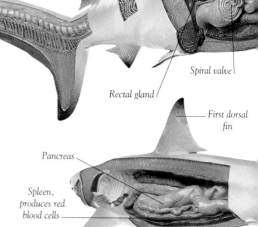

Dorsal fin

Segmented swimming muscles

Spiral valve

Rectal gland

First dorsal fin

Pancreas

Spleen, produces red blood cells

BODY FACTS

• Large olfactory lobes in the brain show how important the sense of smell is to a shark.

• The tongue is supported by a pad of cartilage.

• The gall bladder releases a greenish fluid called bile into the gut that aids digestion.

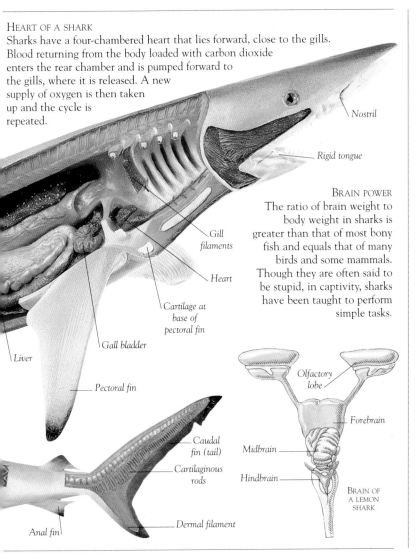

HEART OF A SHARK

Sharks have a four-chambered heart that lies forward, close to the gills. Blood returning from the body loaded with carbon dioxide enters the rear chamber and is pumped forward to the gills, where it is released. A new supply of oxygen is then taken up and the cycle is repeated.

Nostril

Rigid tongue

BRAIN POWER

The ratio of brain weight to body weight in sharks is greater than that of most bony fish and equals that of many birds and some mammals. Though they are often said to be stupid, in captivity, sharks have been taught to perform simple tasks.

Gill filaments

Heart

Cartilage at base of pectoral fin

Gall bladder

Liver

Pectoral fin

Caudal fin (tail)

Cartilaginous rods

Midbrain

Hindbrain

Anal fin

Dermal filament

Olfactory lobe

Forebrain

BRAIN OF A LEMON SHARK

Gills and liver

A shark breathes by taking water into its mouth and pumping it over the gills that lie behind its head. As the water flows past, oxygen in it is removed and passes into the bloodstream to be used in the shark's body. The liver contains high quantities of oil which aid buoyancy – like the swim bladder of a bony fish.

SHUT
As the shark takes water into its mouth (the equivalent of breathing in), the gill slits are closed.

OPEN
Water and carbon dioxide waste are expelled when the gill slits are open.

EATING AND BREATHING
Basking sharks use their gill slits for feeding as well as breathing. Attached to the gill supports are comb-like structures called gill rakers that filter plankton from seawater.

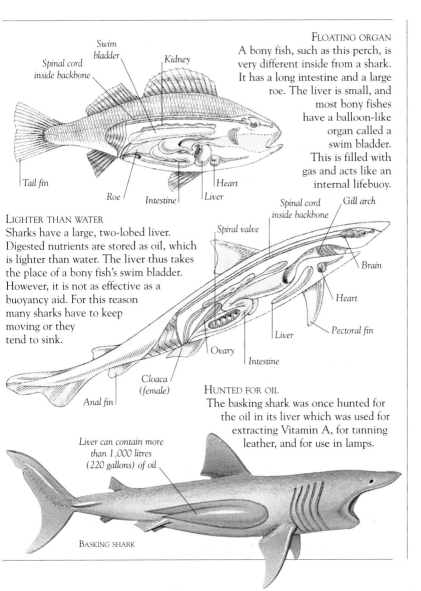

FLOATING ORGAN
A bony fish, such as this perch, is very different inside from a shark. It has a long intestine and a large roe. The liver is small, and most bony fishes have a balloon-like organ called a swim bladder. This is filled with gas and acts like an internal lifebuoy.

Swim bladder
Spinal cord inside backbone
Kidney
Tail fin
Roe
Intestine
Heart
Liver

LIGHTER THAN WATER
Sharks have a large, two-lobed liver. Digested nutrients are stored as oil, which is lighter than water. The liver thus takes the place of a bony fish's swim bladder. However, it is not as effective as a buoyancy aid. For this reason many sharks have to keep moving or they tend to sink.

Spiral valve
Spinal cord inside backbone
Gill arch
Brain
Heart
Liver
Pectoral fin
Ovary
Intestine
Cloaca (female)
Anal fin

HUNTED FOR OIL
The basking shark was once hunted for the oil in its liver which was used for extracting Vitamin A, for tanning leather, and for use in lamps.

Liver can contain more than 1,000 litres (220 gallons) of oil

BASKING SHARK

29

JAWS AND TEETH

SHARKS HAVE UPPER AND LOWER jaws, but unlike most other animals with backbones, their jaws are only loosely attached to the skull. When a shark bites at its prey, the jaws are forced forwards, allowing the teeth to be used more efficiently.

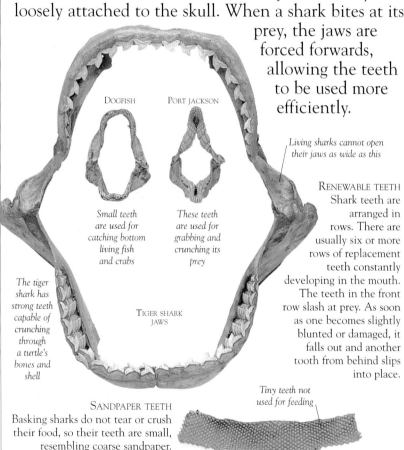

DOGFISH

PORT JACKSON

Living sharks cannot open their jaws as wide as this

RENEWABLE TEETH
Shark teeth are arranged in rows. There are usually six or more rows of replacement teeth constantly developing in the mouth. The teeth in the front row slash at prey. As soon as one becomes slightly blunted or damaged, it falls out and another tooth from behind slips into place.

Small teeth are used for catching bottom living fish and crabs

These teeth are used for grabbing and crunching its prey

The tiger shark has strong teeth capable of crunching through a turtle's bones and shell

TIGER SHARK
JAWS

Tiny teeth not used for feeding

SANDPAPER TEETH
Basking sharks do not tear or crush their food, so their teeth are small, resembling coarse sandpaper.

CRUSHING TEETH

Port Jackson sharks feed on hard-shelled animals without backbones, such as crabs and sea urchins. A pad of small, sharp teeth in the front of their mouths seizes the prey from the seabed. In the back of the jaws is a battery of flat, pebble-like teeth that crushes the armour of their victims.

SECTION THROUGH A PORT JACKSON'S JAWS

BITE-SIZE HOLES

The cookiecutter shark is named after the circular chunks of flesh it bites from its prey. It has small, sharp teeth and feeds on big fish, whales, and seals, all much larger than itself. Cookiecutters shed an entire row of teeth at one time, usually swallowing them with their food.

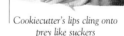

Cookiecutter's lips cling onto prey like suckers

HUNGRY TEETH

The sand tiger raises its overhanging snout as it attacks its prey. Its pointed teeth are ideal for grabbing and holding fish. It has a huge appetite and may eat more than 45 kg (99 lb) of food in a single meal.

31

SKELETONS

SHARKS ARE DIFFERENT from all other animals and humans in that their skeletons contain no bone. Instead, they are made from a soft, flexible, gristly material called cartilage. In some sharks, part of the skeleton is strengthened with calcium salts, particularly in the bones of the back, jaws, and braincase.

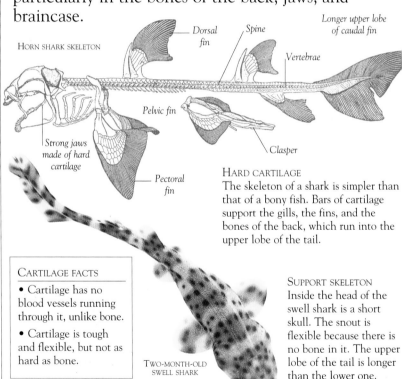

HORN SHARK SKELETON

Dorsal fin

Spine

Longer upper lobe of caudal fin

Vertebrae

Pelvic fin

Strong jaws made of hard cartilage

Clasper

Pectoral fin

TWO-MONTH-OLD SWELL SHARK

HARD CARTILAGE
The skeleton of a shark is simpler than that of a bony fish. Bars of cartilage support the gills, the fins, and the bones of the back, which run into the upper lobe of the tail.

CARTILAGE FACTS

• Cartilage has no blood vessels running through it, unlike bone.

• Cartilage is tough and flexible, but not as hard as bone.

SUPPORT SKELETON
Inside the head of the swell shark is a short skull. The snout is flexible because there is no bone in it. The upper lobe of the tail is longer than the lower one.

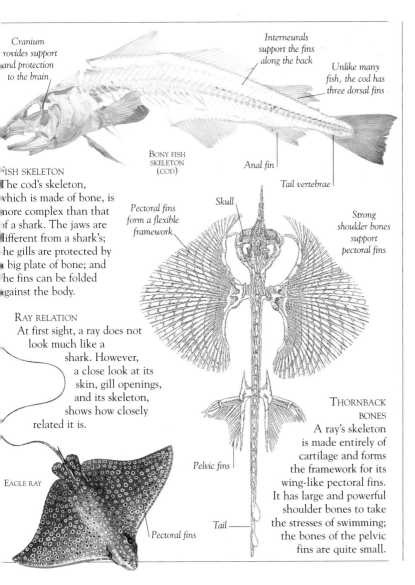

Cranium provides support and protection to the brain

Interneurals support the fins along the back

Unlike many fish, the cod has three dorsal fins

BONY FISH SKELETON (COD)

Anal fin

Tail vertebrae

FISH SKELETON
The cod's skeleton, which is made of bone, is more complex than that of a shark. The jaws are different from a shark's; the gills are protected by a big plate of bone; and the fins can be folded against the body.

RAY RELATION
At first sight, a ray does not look much like a shark. However, a close look at its skin, gill openings, and its skeleton, shows how closely related it is.

EAGLE RAY

Pectoral fins form a flexible framework

Skull

Strong shoulder bones support pectoral fins

Pelvic fins

Pectoral fins

Tail

THORNBACK BONES
A ray's skeleton is made entirely of cartilage and forms the framework for its wing-like pectoral fins. It has large and powerful shoulder bones to take the stresses of swimming; the bones of the pelvic fins are quite small.

33

SKIN

A SHARK'S SKIN is protected, not by scales, but by small, hard, "skin teeth" or dermal denticles. Denticles vary in shape from one part of the body to another. They are rounded on its snout and pointed on its back; in the jaws, the denticles develop into powerful teeth.

19th-century samurai sword

DENTICLES
X 10 MAGNIFICATION

SKIN TEETH
A shark's dermal denticles are covered with enamel. Below the enamel is a layer of dentine, which is the basic material of most teeth. Each dentine layer has a cavity which has a bony base, containing blood vessels and nerves, set deep in the skin.

HARDWEARING DECORATION
The skin of many sharks is used for making leather or a natural type of sandpaper called shagreen. This Japanese samurai sword is enclosed in a sheath of ray skin. The skin has been polished and lacquered so that its denticles are smooth.

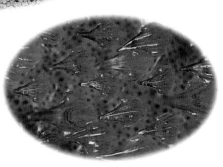

SKIN DETAIL OF LESSER-SPOTTED DOGFISH

It is possible to see growth rings on the scale of a fish which indicate its age

FISH SCALE

SCALE BONES
The scales of a bony fish, such as a salmon or perch, are made of thin slips of bone, set in the skin like the overlapping tiles on a roof. As the fish grows, the scales increase in size.

BRAMBLE SHARK SKIN
A few kinds of shark have very small denticles or even a smooth skin. A bramble shark has scattered denticles, some of which have a tuft of little spikes like the thorns of a blackberry.

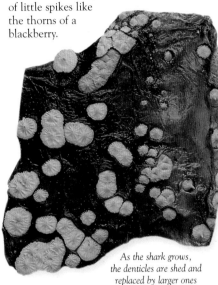

As the shark grows, the denticles are shed and replaced by larger ones

WELL DISGUISED
The wobbegong matches the colour of the seabed on which it lies. Its prey is lured by the fringe of tassels around its mouth. The wobbegong's mouth looks like seaweed to the creatures it eats.

35

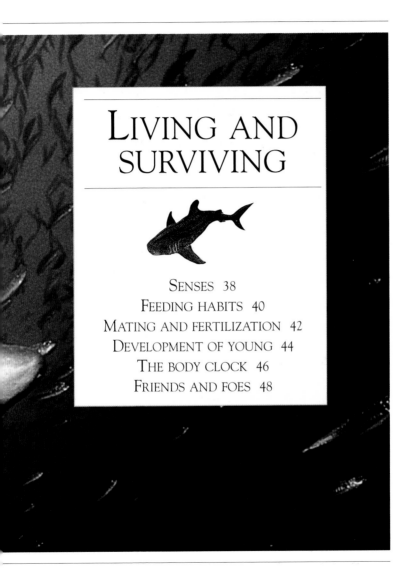

LIVING AND SURVIVING

SENSES

A SHARK'S SENSES tell it about the world in which it lives. Besides being able to see, smell, and hear, a shark can also sense movements and electrical fields made by other animals in the water. Using this sense of "touch", it locates food or enemies. The sharpness of a shark's senses varies from one species to another, depending on lifestyle.

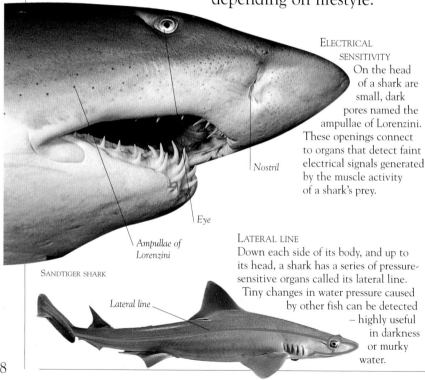

ELECTRICAL SENSITIVITY
On the head of a shark are small, dark pores named the ampullae of Lorenzini. These openings connect to organs that detect faint electrical signals generated by the muscle activity of a shark's prey.

Nostril

Eye

Ampullae of Lorenzini

SANDTIGER SHARK

Lateral line

LATERAL LINE
Down each side of its body, and up to its head, a shark has a series of pressure-sensitive organs called its lateral line. Tiny changes in water pressure caused by other fish can be detected – highly useful in darkness or murky water.

BALANCE MECHANISM

When a shark turns or changes level, liquid moves against the hair-like organs that line the canals of the ear. Ear stones move as the shark changes speed, keeping it informed of position and movement.

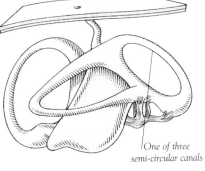

One of three semi-circular canals

Large nostrils of horn shark

SCENT DETECTORS

As a shark swims, water constantly flows into its nostril sacs, which are lined with scent-detecting cells.

EYES

Sharks can see well in dim light. Their eyes have a layer of cells called a tapetum that reflects light back onto the retina. In bright light they can close the pupil to a narrow slit. Some sharks have a light-blocking screen to filter light.

DOGFISH WITH CLOSED PUPIL

HORN SHARK'S PUPIL

RAY EYE WITH SCREEN

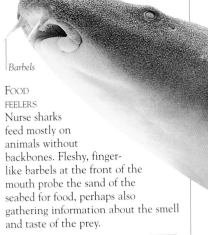

Barbels

FOOD FEELERS

Nurse sharks feed mostly on animals without backbones. Fleshy, finger-like barbels at the front of the mouth probe the sand of the seabed for food, perhaps also gathering information about the smell and taste of the prey.

39

FEEDING HABITS

SHARKS EAT MANY different types of food, but all are flesh eaters. Most eat small fish or invertebrates and some will grab carrion when they can. Three large species filter food, known as plankton, from the sea. Some sharks hunt large animals, including sea lions and other sharks.

GENTLE EATER
The whale shark mainly feeds on plankton. Mesh-like filters sift tiny creatures from the water that passes over its gills. On occasion the whale shark becomes an active hunter, preying on shoals of small fish, such as anchovy.

FEEDING FACTS
• Sharks do not need to feed every day.
• Undigested food may remain in the stomach for several days.
• Smell and the lateral line are the principal senses used by the shark to lead it to food.

SHARP TEETH
The horn shark uses its sense of smell to locate animals such as sea urchins and shellfish on which it feeds. They are caught with its sharp front teeth and crushed with flat teeth in the back of its mouth.

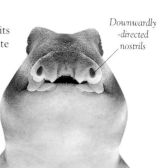

Downwardly -directed nostrils

This shark grows to about 1 m (3 ft)

NIGHT FEEDER
The lesser-spotted dogfish lives near land in water up to 100 m (328 ft) deep. During the day it hides among seaweed. At night it searches for shellfish and small fish.

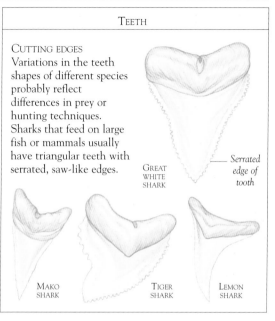

TEETH

CUTTING EDGES
Variations in the teeth shapes of different species probably reflect differences in prey or hunting techniques. Sharks that feed on large fish or mammals usually have triangular teeth with serrated, saw-like edges.

GREAT WHITE SHARK

Serrated edge of tooth

MAKO SHARK

TIGER SHARK

LEMON SHARK

SWIFT HUNTERS
Blue sharks swim fast enough to prey on active fish such as mackerel. They are known as "blue whalers" because they sometimes gather in feeding frenzies around whale carcasses, their favourite food.

Snout turns up as shark attacks

BLUE SHARK WITH PREY

MATING AND FERTILIZATION

WHEN SOME MALE AND FEMALE sharks meet, the male chases and bites the female, encouraging her to mate. Sharks' mating behaviour ensures that, unlike bony fish, the eggs are fertilized inside the female. In some species, the female lays eggs; in others, the young develop inside their mother – while some sharks are capable of both.

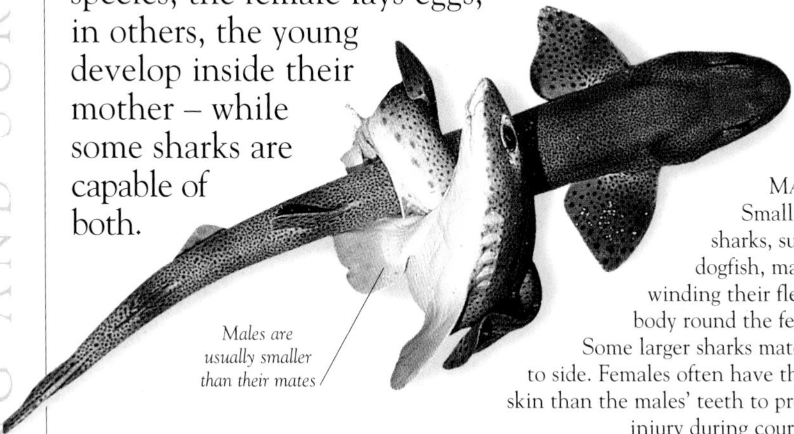

Males are usually smaller than their mates

MATING
Small male sharks, such as dogfish, mate by winding their flexible body round the female. Some larger sharks mate side to side. Females often have thicker skin than the males' teeth to prevent injury during courtship.

REPRODUCTIVE ORGANS
Male sharks have a pair of claspers that are formed from part of the pelvic fins. During mating one of them is inserted into the female opening, named the cloaca. Sperm is released into the female to fertilize the eggs.

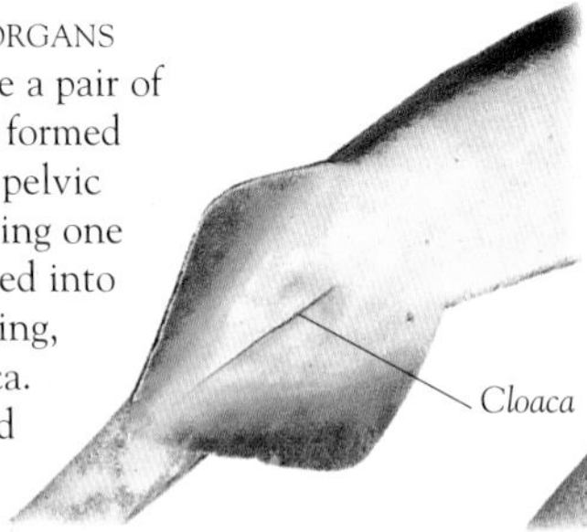

Cloaca

Clasper

FEMALE PELVIC FINS

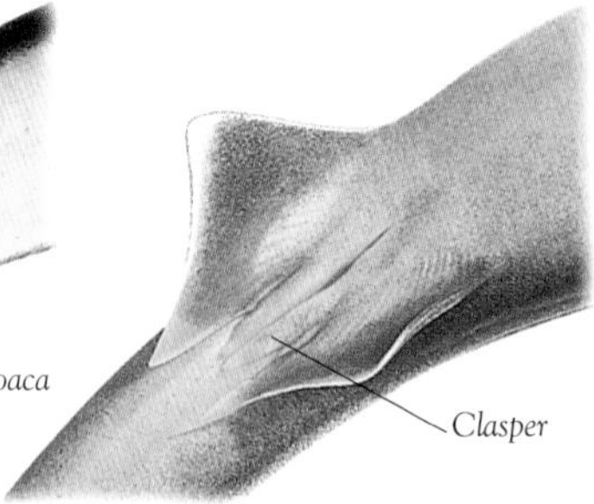

MALE PELVIC FINS

EGG CASES

Shark eggs have a large egg yolk that is protected in a horny or leathery case. Female horn sharks lay spiral egg cases which they wedge into clefts in rocks for safety from other creatures.

Embryo dogfish inside an egg case

SPIRAL EGG CASE
OF HORN SHARK

EMBRYO DEVELOPMENT

Sharks take up to a year to develop. When a pup hatches, it is at least 10 cm (4 in) long. As a result, it stands a better chance of survival than one of the many tiny young produced by most bony fish.

The embryo is nourished with a large yolk sac

HIDING PLACE

Most dogfish lay their eggs in dense beds of seaweed. The curly, ribbon-like ends on the corners of the egg cases tangle with seaweed fronds and are held safely. The movement of the water brings oxygen to the developing embryo.

MATING AND FERTILIZATION

DEVELOPMENT OF YOUNG

IN SOME SHARKS, the female produces thin-shelled eggs, which remain inside her body until they hatch. Sometimes baby sharks hatch at an early stage, but do not leave their mother's body. Each one continues to grow, feeding on its egg's large yolk sac.

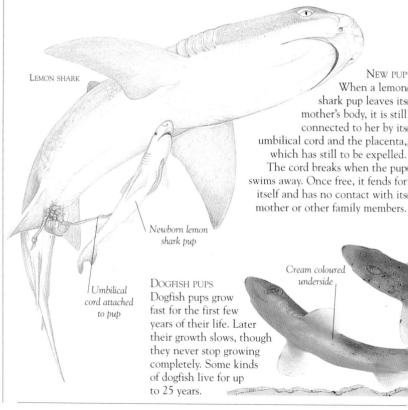

LEMON SHARK

Newborn lemon shark pup

Umbilical cord attached to pup

NEW PUP
When a lemon shark pup leaves its mother's body, it is still connected to her by its umbilical cord and the placenta, which has still to be expelled. The cord breaks when the pup swims away. Once free, it fends for itself and has no contact with its mother or other family members.

Cream coloured underside

DOGFISH PUPS
Dogfish pups grow fast for the first few years of their life. Later their growth slows, though they never stop growing completely. Some kinds of dogfish live for up to 25 years.

BIRTH FOR SURVIVAL

Birth is usually a rapid process to protect the newborn pup from enemies waiting to take advantage of a female or young in difficulty. Remoras are often nearby, waiting for the afterbirth, which they eat quickly. This reduces the likelihood of predators – including other sharks – being attracted to the birth scene.

TAIL FIRST

As a precaution against complications during birth, sharks are born tail first. The pup stands a better chance of survival if its head is still protected by its mother's body.

ENDANGERED NEWBORN

Game fishermen deliberately pursue female sharks as they are generally larger than males. Sometimes the trauma of being caught results in the female giving birth early to a litter of pups.

Pair of dogfish pups 10 days old and 10 cm (4 in) long

Soon the pups will feed on small creatures, such as shrimps

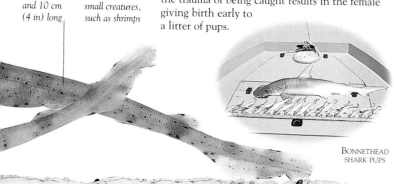

BONNETHEAD
SHARK PUPS

THE BODY CLOCK

ALL ANIMALS LIVE to rhythms dictated by the sun and the seasons. These are translated into patterns of behaviour such as sleeping, breeding, or migrating. Even the lives of deep-sea sharks are regulated by their body clocks.

SLEEPER
SHARK
It used to be thought that sharks had to swim in order to breathe, but this is not true. The greenland shark and its close relatives are known as "sleeper sharks" because as well as being generally inactive, they spend a lot of time on the seabed, apparently asleep.

The greenland shark is a deep-water "sleeper"

SLEEPING FACTS

• Dreaming has been observed in bony fish, but not yet in sharks.

• The basking shark is probably the only plankton eater that hibernates. The others live where the food supply is less seasonal.

WINTER DOZE
In winter, when the supply of plankton falls, basking sharks hibernate. A number have been caught in trawls, and when examined found to have lost their gill rakers. New ones grow for the spring flush of plankton.

FAST ASLEEP

Nurse sharks are among several kinds of reef sharks known to rest for long periods on the sea floor. They appear to be breathing slowly, but if disturbed will swim off in a flurry as though woken from a deep sleep.

BLUE SHARK

Blue sharks do not sleep on the seabed

MIGRATION RHYTHM

Blue sharks migrate each year, moving between breeding and feeding grounds at definite times of the year. Like other oceanic sharks, blue sharks may rest without sinking to the bottom.

GREATEST TRAVELLER
Tagging, mainly in the US, has shown that some blue sharks cover more than 6,000 km (3,726 miles) a year. More work remains to be done before the movements of different populations can be fully understood.

RELEASE OF BLUE SHARKS

TAGGING RELEASE AREAS OFF US COAST

TAGGING RELEASE AREAS ELSEWHERE

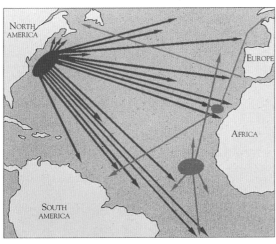

NORTH AMERICA

EUROPE

AFRICA

SOUTH AMERICA

FRIENDS AND FOES

SHARKS HAVE FEW natural enemies, but many creatures known as commensals live near to, or are attached to, large sharks. Some of these creatures are able to live without the shark, unlike parasites such as tapeworms, which cannot survive away from their host's body.

Tentacle

Head

Suction pad

REMORAS
Remoras are sometimes called "shark suckers" because they attach themselves to a shark with a ridged sucker on top of their heads. They may feed on the shark's food scraps and are thought to aid the shark by also feeding on tiny parasites lodged in its skin.

TAPEWORMS
Inside the gut of a shark live hundreds of parasites called tapeworms. They feed on digested food and can grow up to 30 cm (1 ft) long.

PILOT FISH
In tropical waters, agile pilot fish swim below sharks. They do not, as their name suggests, guide the shark, but benefit from the protection gained by travelling with large sharks.

SKIN FEEDERS

Copepods are small relatives of crabs and form part of the plankton of the sea. Some become parasites on a shark's skin or gills, attaching themselves with adhesive pads and feeding on skin secretions.

FEMALE COPEPOD   MALE COPEPOD

EYE SPY

This crustacean is a parasite that feeds on the surface of the eyes of greenland sharks. It may damage its host's vision, but may also attract small fish for the shark to eat.

Egg sac contains thousands of eggs

EYE SPY

SHARP CLAWS

This copepod hangs on to the shark's skin, feeding partly on blood. Basking sharks are thought to rid themselves of the irritation by leaping out of the sea.

Abdomen

Soft shell

HANGERS ON

Many large oceanic animals carry barnacles. The rootlets on the fleshy stalk of this barnacle feed on the shark's body fluids.

BARNACLE

DOLPHIN VERSUS SHARK

It is thought that dolphins drive sharks away, but this is not necessarily true. However, the bottlenose dolphin has been trained by scientists in Florida, US, to chase and attack sharks. During these experiments, the dolphin appeared able to distinguish one shark species from another.

When sharks and dolphins share an aquarium, they usually ignore each other

BOTTLENOSE DOLPHIN

FRIENDS AND FOES

49

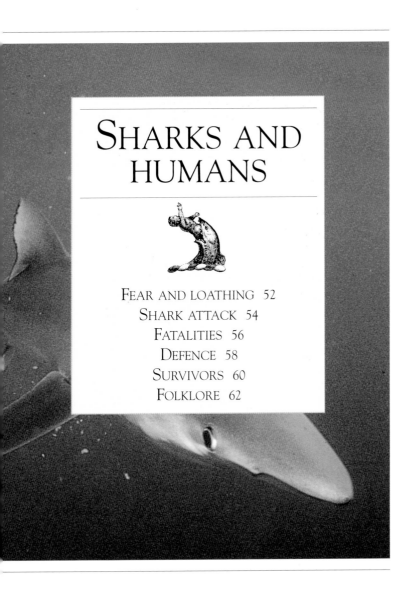

SHARKS AND HUMANS

FEAR AND LOATHING

THE SHARK IS A POWERFUL symbol of terror, and sharks have traditionally been regarded as fearsome sea beasts to be hunted and killed without mercy. Sailors once believed that sharks preferred human flesh to all other and, even today, many regard all sharks as potential maneaters.

HOLLYWOOD PARANOIA
The 1975 film *Jaws*, about a "killer" great white shark, scared audiences out of the water, and fuelled worldwide hatred and fear of sharks. However, Peter Benchley, the author of the novel *Jaws*, now supports shark conservation.

ARTIST'S IMPRESSION
This engraving of a shark cast onto a beach in France was created more than 100 years ago. The mixture of features in the illustration – size of a great white, tail shape of a thresher – suggests that the artist was working from a description, not life.

FEEDING FRENZY

This shipwreck was the front cover of a Paris magazine in 1906. It illustrated one of sailors' most common fears – that of sharks in a feeding frenzy, swarming round a sinking ship, picking off survivors one by one.

TERRIBLE DRAME EN MER — NAUFRAGÉS ATTAQUÉS PAR DES REQUINS

SANTA MARIA

Columbus sailed this ship

BAD OMEN

Disease was common among early explorers, and dead bodies were often thrown overboard, which sometimes attracted sharks. Superstitious sailors believed that the presence of sharks foretold further deaths.

SHIPWRECK CASUALTIES CAUSED BY SHARKS

Tragedies at sea are a rare occurence, but are made much worse by sharks. During World War II, many lives were lost when sharks closed in on wounded and struggling sailors.

SHIP	DATE	PASSENGERS AND CREW	NUMBER LOST
Valerian	1926	104	84
Principessa Mafalda	1927	1,259	314
Cape San Juan	1943	1,429	981
Indianapolis	1945	1,199	883
Ganges Ferry Boat	1975	190	50+

SUPERSTITION FACTS

• Sailors falsely believed that sharks preferred the taste of people of their own nationality.

• Sailors used to take revenge on any shark they caught by torturing it to death.

SHARK ATTACK

NOBODY KNOWS why sharks sometimes attack people; most sharks are not dangerous and ignore humans unless threatened or provoked. Experts are unable to agree on the number of deaths caused by sharks.

Outer plastic casing

Casing of steel laths

Stainless steel ball bearings

Aluminium core

SHALLOW WATER
Attacks on humans often take place close to the shore in shallow water. This is probably because the majority of people are found swimming and paddling in this area.

BITE METER
By measuring the depth of the indentations when this device is placed inside a piece of bait, it is possible to determine the strength of a shark's bite.

MISTAKEN IDENTITY
More men than women fall victim to shark attack. The reason for this is likely to be that men are more likely to swim alone in deep water. More men than women surf, and sharks can easily mistake a surfer for a seal, which is part of their natural diet.

SEAL FROM BELOW

SURFBOARD RIDER

PUBLIC ENEMY

The tiger shark is large and powerful enough to attack most sea creatures. Its diet includes seals, dolphins, sea snakes, hammerhead sharks, and turtles. Many humans have been killed by this shark.

RIVER MENACE

Bull sharks are dreaded in many parts of the tropics because they venture up rivers, posing a real threat to wildlife and humans alike.

GREAT HUNTER

The great white is deservedly the most feared shark of all. It can swim fast enough to jump clean out of the water and is large enough to attack any animal in the sea. It has even been known to attack and sink small boats.

Fatalities

A person is more likely to be struck by lightning than attacked by a shark. Although experts disagree, it has been suggested that since 1940, there have been an average of only 28 attacks each year, one-third of which were fatal, worldwide. These figures include attacks made by sharks in self defence or by those that were caught or harrassed in some way.

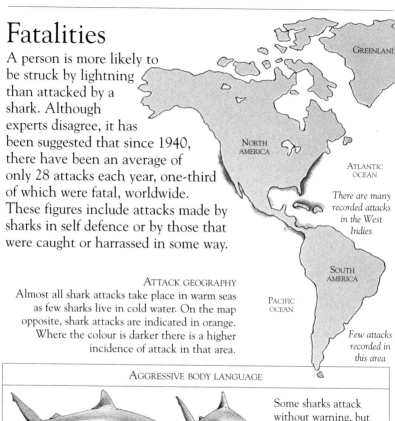

GREENLAND

NORTH AMERICA

ATLANTIC OCEAN

There are many recorded attacks in the West Indies

SOUTH AMERICA

PACIFIC OCEAN

Few attacks recorded in this area

ATTACK GEOGRAPHY
Almost all shark attacks take place in warm seas as few sharks live in cold water. On the map opposite, shark attacks are indicated in orange. Where the colour is darker there is a higher incidence of attack in that area.

AGGRESSIVE BODY LANGUAGE

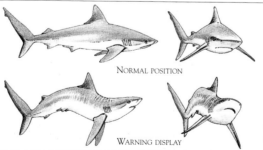

NORMAL POSITION

WARNING DISPLAY

Some sharks attack without warning, but the grey reef shark warns intruders. It displays a threatening posture by raising its snout and lowering its pectoral fins. If a diver does not retreat, the shark will attack.

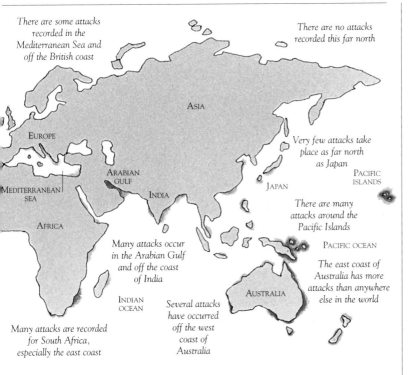

There are some attacks recorded in the Mediterranean Sea and off the British coast

There are no attacks recorded this far north

ASIA

Very few attacks take place as far north as Japan

PACIFIC ISLANDS

EUROPE

JAPAN

ARABIAN GULF

MEDITERRANEAN SEA

INDIA

There are many attacks around the Pacific Islands

AFRICA

PACIFIC OCEAN

Many attacks occur in the Arabian Gulf and off the coast of India

The east coast of Australia has more attacks than anywhere else in the world

AUSTRALIA

INDIAN OCEAN

Several attacks have occurred off the west coast of Australia

Many attacks are recorded for South Africa, especially the east coast

FATAL ATTACKS

More people now survive close encounters with sharks because of faster and better medical attention. These statistics are from an Australian analysis of fatalities in shallow seas.

Each year an average of 92 per cent of deaths are due to drowning…

…about eight per cent are killed scuba diving

…and less than one per cent dies from shark attack

SOUND ADVICE

• Do not swim at dusk or after dark when sharks may be feeding.

• Beware if there are unusually large amounts of fish nearby.

• Bait from fishing boats may attract sharks.

DEFENCE

ALL KINDS OF DEVICES – nets, repellents, electrical barriers, air bubbles – have been specially designed to protect swimmers and divers from the dangers of shark attack. Few, if any, have proved entirely successful, and some have proved dangerous to other sea creatures.

SHARK NET
Popular bathing beaches are often secured against sharks with mesh nets. Nets are costly and need constant maintenance, and unfortunately also trap many harmless creatures such as turtles, rays, and dolphins.

ARMOUR SUIT
Some divers at risk from large, active sharks wear protective suits made of steel mesh, like medieval chain-mail armour. The suit prevents a shark's teeth from penetrating the diver's body, though there may be severe bruising from the shark's jaws.

DETAIL OF SHARK SUIT WITH TOOTH
OF GREAT WHITE

CAGE PROTECTION
Some of the most dramatic pictures of sharks have been shot by underwater film makers enclosed by stout, metal cages. A shark's ability to detect underwater electric fields has possibly been the cause of numerous attacks on cages.

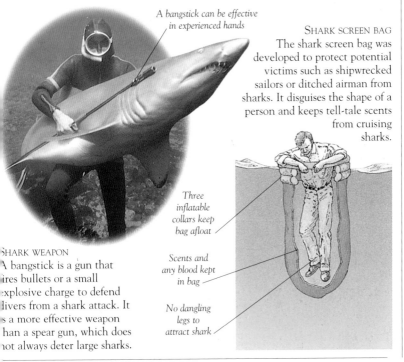

A bangstick can be effective in experienced hands

SHARK SCREEN BAG
The shark screen bag was developed to protect potential victims such as shipwrecked sailors or ditched airman from sharks. It disguises the shape of a person and keeps tell-tale scents from cruising sharks.

Three inflatable collars keep bag afloat

Scents and any blood kept in bag

No dangling legs to attract shark

SHARK WEAPON
A bangstick is a gun that fires bullets or a small explosive charge to defend divers from a shark attack. It is a more effective weapon than a spear gun, which does not always deter large sharks.

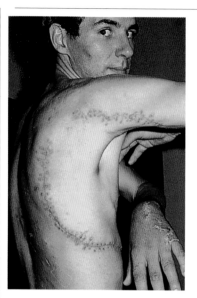

SURVIVORS

SHARK ATTACKS are by no means all fatal. However, most survivors have been physically fit and have remained calm during the attack. They have also been swimming near friends or within reach of a boat. Some people have survived by fighting back – attacking the shark's eyes with their bare hands.

MIRACULOUS RECOVERY

Australian diver, Rodney Fox, was taking part in spear fishing competition near Adelaide in 1963 when he was attacked by a great white shark. His upper body was badly crushed and torn. He was rushed to hospital where he received 462 stitches in a 4-hour operation.

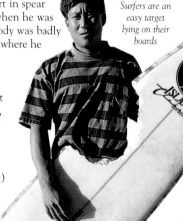

Surfers are an easy target lying on their boards

SURVIVAL FACTS

- Most sharks will only strike once.

- Blood loss and shock are the most dangerous effects of shark bites.

- About one-quarter of all attacks kill the victim.

LUCKY ESCAPE

Surfers can be at risk from sharks, athough few are attacked. This surfer's board was bitten by a 3–4 m (10–13 ft) shark near a coral reef in Hawaii, US.

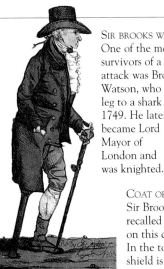

SIR BROOKS WATSON

One of the most famous survivors of a shark attack was Brooks Watson, who lost a leg to a shark in 1749. He later became Lord Mayor of London and was knighted.

Neptune, Roman god of the sea

COAT OF ARMS

Sir Brooks Watson recalled his history on this coat of arms. In the top left of the shield is his severed leg.

The motto means "Under God's shield"

CLOSE CALL

Valerie Taylor is a shark expert who has watched and filmed sharks for many years. In the photograph above she has been bitten on the leg. She was not seriously injured, but still needed hospital treatment.

FORGIVING DIVER

Henri Bource lost a leg off the coast of Australia, where he was attacked by a great white in 1964. He still dives and does not blame the shark for its natural behaviour.

FOLKLORE

THE INHABITANTS of some Pacific islands regard certain sharks as gods, or spirits of their ancestors. Ancient Polynesians often believed that sharks were spirits sent by sorcerers to bring death and ill fortune. In some parts of West Africa, the shark is sacred and if one is accidentally killed, sacrificial rites must be performed.

SHARK/
BONITO
This charm, from Ulawa in the Solomon Islands is of a bonito fish on one side, and a shark on the other. Hunters carried carvings like these in their canoes hoping to attract the bonito and repel large sharks.

The bonito hunting ritual was an annual event

Carving made of wood, inlaid with pearl

Shark-like head

LATE 19TH-CENTURY SHARK CHARM

FOLKLORE FACTS

• Some Pacific Islanders believed that sharks would protect and save them from drowning.

• In northern Borneo, to stop babies crying, the saw from a sawfish is covered in cloth and hung over the cradle.

SEA SPIRIT
Solomon Islanders believed that when people died their ghosts inhabited the bodies of sharks. This sea spirit has a head with fins like a shark. It was probably used to protect its maker from danger when fishing at sea.

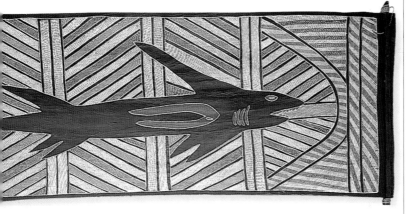

SHARK PAINTING
This painting of a shark by the Yirrakala
people of the Northern Territory,
Australia, shows the huge two-lobed
liver. Sharks were important to many
native people as a source of food and oil.

*Early 20th-century
rattle from Papua
New Guinea for
attracting sharks*

*Rattle
made
from
coconut
shells*

SHARK MASK
Native Americans
from Alaska carve
animal masks for
use on ceremonial
occasions. This
mask is of a ground
shark with a frog
in its mouth.
It is made of
painted wood
and leather,
inlaid with
abalone
shell.

RATTLES
Some Pacific
Islanders hunt sharks
as a test of strength
and manhood,
others use the shark
skin and teeth for
decoration and
weapons. The
shark is lured
using underwater
rattles.

SHARK DIRECTORY

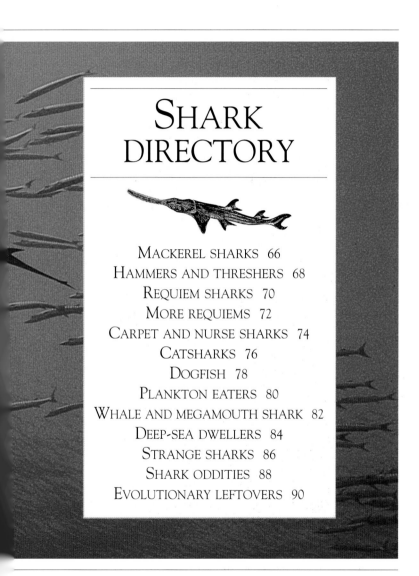

MACKEREL SHARKS

THE GREAT WHITE, the porbeagle, and the mako are collectively known as mackerel sharks. Powerful, fast swimmers, they feed on many kinds of prey. They are all able to push their jaws forwards, to tear chunks from prey too large to be swallowed whole. Little is known about their breeding behaviour or migratory habits.

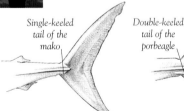

GREAT WHITE

WARM-BLOODED

Porbeagle sharks prefer more temperate seas and may be seen near the British and North American coasts in summer. They are heavily built and partly warm-blooded, being able to keep their body temperature several degrees higher than their surroundings.

MACKEREL FACTS

• Mackerel sharks make spectacular leaps when hooked by game fishermen.

• Unborn makos and porbeagles survive in the uterus by eating the unfertilized eggs.

• Normally only two pups are born at a time.

Single-keeled tail of the mako

Double-keeled tail of the porbeagle

TAIL FINS

The tail lobes of mackerel sharks are nearly equal in size. Mako and porbeagles have small stabilizing keels at the base of their tail. The keel probably helps the fish to keep on course when making tight turns.

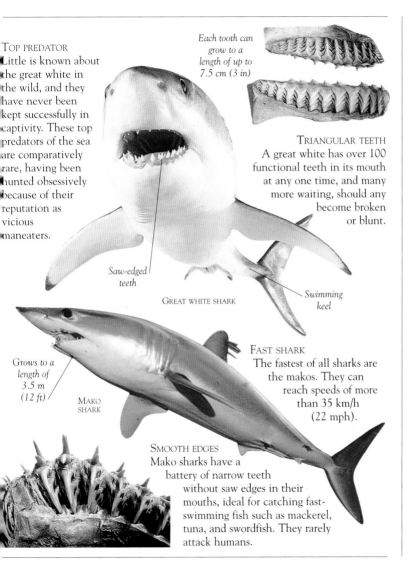

TOP PREDATOR

Little is known about the great white in the wild, and they have never been kept successfully in captivity. These top predators of the sea are comparatively rare, having been hunted obsessively because of their reputation as vicious maneaters.

Each tooth can grow to a length of up to 7.5 cm (3 in)

TRIANGULAR TEETH

A great white has over 100 functional teeth in its mouth at any one time, and many more waiting, should any become broken or blunt.

Saw-edged teeth

GREAT WHITE SHARK

Swimming keel

Grows to a length of 3.5 m (12 ft)

MAKO SHARK

FAST SHARK

The fastest of all sharks are the makos. They can reach speeds of more than 35 km/h (22 mph).

SMOOTH EDGES

Mako sharks have a battery of narrow teeth without saw edges in their mouths, ideal for catching fast-swimming fish such as mackerel, tuna, and swordfish. They rarely attack humans.

HAMMERS AND THRESHERS

THE HAMMERHEAD and the thresher shark are not
closely related, but both are easy to recognize; one for
its extraordinary head, the other for its long tail,
which may make up half its length. The teeth of close
relatives of hammerheads and thresher sharks have
been found in rocks at least 60 million years old.

LONG TAIL
Most threshers are surface
swimmers, hunting small fish
such as herring or pilchard.
Thresher pups may be 1.5 m
(5 ft) long at birth. One
species has very large eyes
and lives in deep water.

*Upper lobe
of tail may
be half the
size of body*

*Can grow up
to 6 m
(20 ft) long*

*Threshers
weigh about
450 kg
(1,000 lb)*

THRESHER
SHARK

BONNET HEAD
The shovel-shaped head, with eyes and
nostrils on the outer edge, marks the
bonnet shark as a small relative of the great
hammerheads. It often comes into
shallow bays to hunt small
fish, crabs, and shrimps.
Like all hammerheads, it
produces live young.

Gill slits

BONNET SHARK

*Mouth is located under
the head*

SENSORY HEAD

Hammerheads swing their heads from side to side as they swim, testing the water for the presence of stingrays, their main prey. Sometimes the sting of a ray will become embedded in a shark's jaws, causing its teeth to grow abnormally.

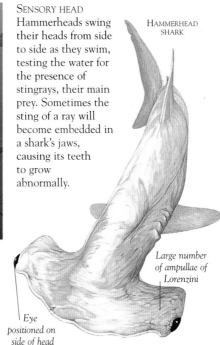

HAMMERHEAD SHARK

Large number of ampullae of Lorenzini

Eye positioned on side of head

HAMMER SCHOOLS

Hammerheads hunt as individuals at night, and by day swim together in large numbers. In such a school, there are about four females to every male, but nobody has ever observed hammerheads mating.

LETHAL TAIL

Thresher sharks are thought to work in pairs, lashing their tails to frighten groups of fish into a tight pack that can be caught easily. Threshers are sought after by game fishermen as they are exciting prey. However, they can inflict severe injuries with their powerful tail.

REQUIEM SHARKS

SAILORS IN DAYS GONE BY did not name this group of sharks because of any connection with death. They called them requiem or "rest" sharks because they were often seen in fair weather. Some requiems live in the open ocean while others, such as those shown here, are found close to the shore.

WARNING SIGNAL

Divers may encounter grey reef sharks as they are often found in lagoons and on the outer edges of reefs. They are not usually dangerous, but may be territorial. If it feels threatened, a grey reef shark will warn intruders by arching its back into an aggressive posture.

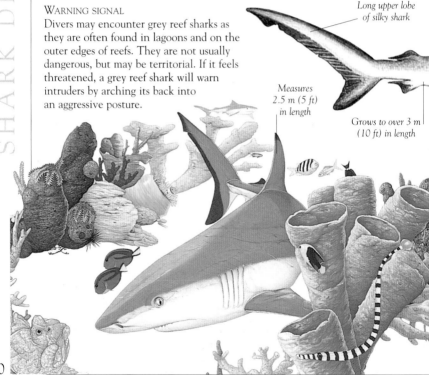

Long upper lobe of silky shark

Measures 2.5 m (5 ft) in length

Grows to over 3 m (10 ft) in length

LAGOON DWELLER

The lemon shark is often found in shallow lagoons. It eats crabs, octopuses, and sea birds. It also eats stingrays, and often has stings embedded in its mouth as a result. It is born in shallow water where it stays for some years before gradually venturing out into open seas.

LEMON SHARK

SILKY SMOOTH

SILKY SHARK

Named because of its small and smooth dermal denticles, the silky shark's sides do not have the rough feel of those of most other sharks. It is one of the most common species of shark, often taking tuna from the nets of fishermen.

Dorsal fin sticks out of the water in shallows

Body length can reach 1.8 m (6 ft)

Denticles of silky shark are only 0.25 mm (0.01 in) across

REQUIEM FACTS

• Females store their mate's sperm until the next year, when the eggs are fertilized.

• Requiems produce about 14 young in a litter.

• Requiem pups grow faster than other sharks.

AGGRESSIVE SPECIES

Often lying in reef pools only 60 cm (2 ft) deep, blacktip reef sharks are not to be trifled with. They can become aggressive if they detect fishing bait, and may attack people.

71

More requiems

The requiem sharks shown here are all large species that may be dangerous. The blue shark lives in almost all the oceans of the world and is responsible for some attacks on shipwrecked sailors. Tiger sharks are only found in warm seas, close to the shore. Bull sharks sometimes venture into fresh water.

BLUE SHARK

TRAVELLING HUNTER
Blue sharks are the great travellers of the shark world, covering huge distances each year. They do not dive deeply for food, but hunt almost any kind of surface-living fish. They particularly like whale meat and are known to gather in feeding frenzies when they find a whale carcass.

REQUIEM FACTS

• The distinctive stripes on a tiger shark fade as the shark ages.

• Female blue sharks have skin thicker than the length of the male's teeth to prevent injury during courtship.

OCEANIC WHITETIP SHARK

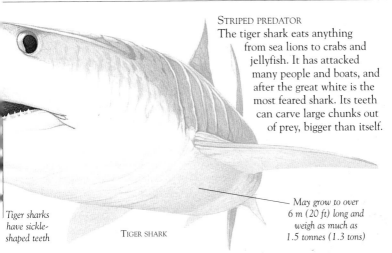

STRIPED PREDATOR

The tiger shark eats anything from sea lions to crabs and jellyfish. It has attacked many people and boats, and after the great white is the most feared shark. Its teeth can carve large chunks out of prey, bigger than itself.

Tiger sharks have sickle-shaped teeth

TIGER SHARK

May grow to over 6 m (20 ft) long and weigh as much as 1.5 tonnes (1.3 tons)

ADAPTABILITY

Bull sharks have developed an ability to maintain a balance between the salt content of their bodies and the fresh water of a river or lake system. Some bull sharks may spend a large portion of their lives in fresh water.

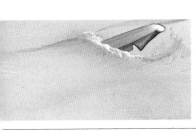

WHITE-TIPPED SHARK

The oceanic whitetip shark is a slow-moving, abundant species that grows to a length of 4 m (13 ft). It is a fearless and very dangerous species found in most parts of the world. This shark is despised by tuna fishermen and whalers because of the harm it inflicts on their catches.

CARPET AND NURSE SHARKS

MOST KINDS OF CARPET and nurse sharks live in Australia and eastern Asiatic waters. They live on the seabed and all are sluggish swimmers. Most are small, with sharp teeth for eating small fish and invertebrates. Nurse sharks were named by early explorers after an ancient word meaning "big fish".

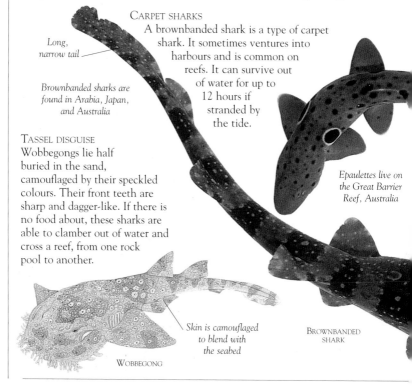

CARPET SHARKS
A brownbanded shark is a type of carpet shark. It sometimes ventures into harbours and is common on reefs. It can survive out of water for up to 12 hours if stranded by the tide.

Long, narrow tail

Brownbanded sharks are found in Arabia, Japan, and Australia

Epaulettes live on the Great Barrier Reef, Australia

TASSEL DISGUISE
Wobbegongs lie half buried in the sand, camouflaged by their speckled colours. Their front teeth are sharp and dagger-like. If there is no food about, these sharks are able to clamber out of water and cross a reef, from one rock pool to another.

Skin is camouflaged to blend with the seabed

BROWNBANDED SHARK

WOBBEGONG

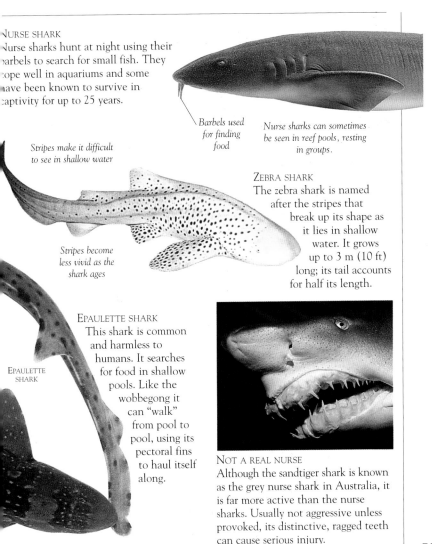

NURSE SHARK

Nurse sharks hunt at night using their barbels to search for small fish. They cope well in aquariums and some have been known to survive in captivity for up to 25 years.

Barbels used for finding food

Nurse sharks can sometimes be seen in reef pools, resting in groups.

Stripes make it difficult to see in shallow water

Stripes become less vivid as the shark ages

ZEBRA SHARK

The zebra shark is named after the stripes that break up its shape as it lies in shallow water. It grows up to 3 m (10 ft) long; its tail accounts for half its length.

EPAULETTE SHARK

This shark is common and harmless to humans. It searches for food in shallow pools. Like the wobbegong it can "walk" from pool to pool, using its pectoral fins to haul itself along.

EPAULETTE
SHARK

NOT A REAL NURSE

Although the sandtiger shark is known as the grey nurse shark in Australia, it is far more active than the nurse sharks. Usually not aggressive unless provoked, its distinctive, ragged teeth can cause serious injury.

CATSHARKS

ONE-THIRD of all sharks belong to the catshark family. Small, slender fish, with two dorsal fins set well back on the body, most are found in deep water where they live on the seabed. A few kinds are known from only one specimen, and it is likely that more will be discovered in the future.

First dorsal fin is placed well back on the body

Does not have a nictitating eyelid (see page 116)

Only about 50 cm (20 in) in length

LONGNOSE CATSHARK

Very long tail fin

DEEP-SEA SHARK
The longnose catshark lives off the west coast of North America. It is a deep-water species that has been recorded as deep as 1,900 m (6,250 ft), but is rarely found above 900 m (3,000 ft). Many deep-sea catsharks are brownish in colour so are well camouflaged for their murky environment.

Grows to about 90 cm (3 ft) long

Blotchy skin and black-banded neck

VARIED CATSHARK
This bottom-living catshark prefers a sandy seabed and is related to the carpet sharks. It is not often seen, though it is occasionally caught in lobster traps.

VARIED CATSHARK

Lives at depths of 160 m (526 ft)

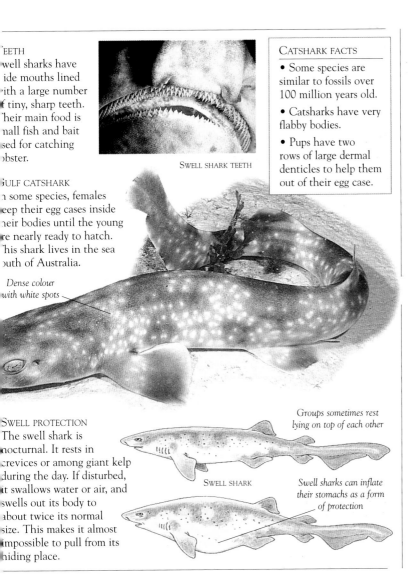

TEETH
Swell sharks have wide mouths lined with a large number of tiny, sharp teeth. Their main food is small fish and bait used for catching lobster.

SWELL SHARK TEETH

CATSHARK FACTS

• Some species are similar to fossils over 100 million years old.

• Catsharks have very flabby bodies.

• Pups have two rows of large dermal denticles to help them out of their egg case.

GULF CATSHARK
In some species, females keep their egg cases inside their bodies until the young are nearly ready to hatch. This shark lives in the sea south of Australia.

Dense colour with white spots

SWELL PROTECTION
The swell shark is nocturnal. It rests in crevices or among giant kelp during the day. If disturbed, it swallows water or air, and swells out its body to about twice its normal size. This makes it almost impossible to pull from its hiding place.

Groups sometimes rest lying on top of each other

SWELL SHARK

Swell sharks can inflate their stomachs as a form of protection

77

DOGFISH

MANY KINDS OF SMALL sharks are known as dogfish.
Some, like the spiny dogfish, are related to deep-water
sharks. They live near the seabed, often close to
land, but have been known to venture into
fresh water, travelling a short distance up
rivers. Dogfish are an important
source of food and are fished
throughout the world.

*Grows to about
2 m (7 ft) in
length*

*Some species
emit an
unpleasant smell*

*Feeds on
bottom-living
invertebrates*

Sharp nose

TOPE

*Can live for
over 40 years*

TOPE
During summer
tope live in
small groups
and the
females may give birth to as many
as 50 pups. Tope are not fished
commercially, but some anglers
specialize in catching them – there
are even tope clubs.

COMMON SPECIES
The lesser-spotted dogfish is one
of the most common sharks in
western European seas. It is
found on sand banks where
there are plenty of sheltering
seaweeds. The females
lay their egg capsules
among the weed to
keep them safe.

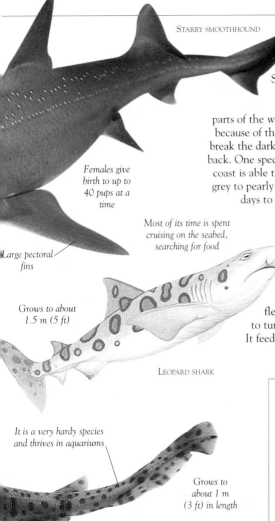

STARRY SMOOTH
Starry smoothhounds are
sluggish sharks that live
in shallow seas in many
parts of the world. They are so named
because of the small, white spots that
break the dark shade of their sides and
back. One species that lives off the US
coast is able to change its colour from
grey to pearly white, taking about two
days to complete the transition.

*Females give
birth to up to
40 pups at a
time*

*Most of its time is spent
cruising on the seabed,
searching for food*

*Large pectoral
fins*

*Grows to about
1.5 m (5 ft)*

LEOPARD SHARK

SPOTTED SKIN
The leopard shark
gets its name from
its golden, blotched
skin. Like some other
carpet sharks, it has a
flexible body that allows it
to turn round in small spaces.
It feeds mainly on clams, using
its flat-topped teeth.

*It is a very hardy species
and thrives in aquariums*

*Grows to
about 1 m
(3 ft) in length*

LESSER-SPOTTED
DOGFISH

DOGFISH FACTS

• Dogfish were
named by fishermen
who thought their
teeth resembled
those of dogs.

• Dogfish are sold
for food in Europe
as rock salmon or
huss, and in Australia
as flake.

79

PLANKTON EATERS

THE THREE LARGEST FISH in the sea – the whale shark, basking shark, and megamouth shark – are all harmless, docile creatures that feed mainly on plankton. All have more than a thousand gill rakers that strain the current for food and an immense liver that contains a substantial amount of oil.

SEA SOUP

Plankton is made up of floating plants and animals that are unable to swim against the ocean currents. A few of these animals, such as jellyfish, may be big, but most are tiny. Some, such as the larvae of crabs and sea urchins, are only part of the plankton "soup" for a short time before growing into adult animals.

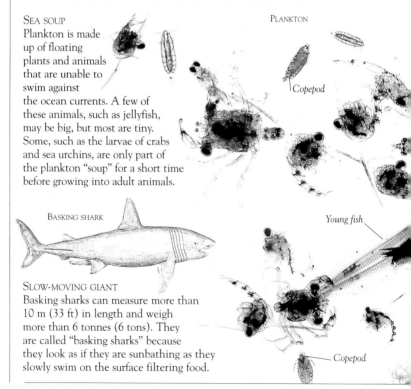

PLANKTON

Copepod

Young fish

Copepod

BASKING SHARK

SLOW-MOVING GIANT

Basking sharks can measure more than 10 m (33 ft) in length and weigh more than 6 tonnes (6 tons). They are called "basking sharks" because they look as if they are sunbathing as they slowly swim on the surface filtering food.

INSIDE THE MOUTH

Basking sharks use the same action to feed and to breathe. Bars of cartilage in the throat support the gills and gill rakers. Water flows into the mouth, where it is drained through the gill rakers to filter out food particles. It is then pushed over the gills, where oxygen and carbon dioxide are exchanged.

BASKING SHARK

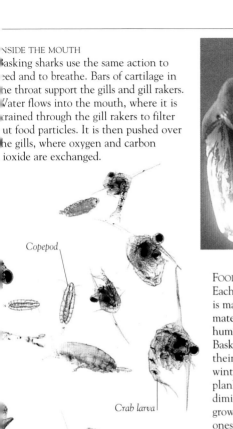

Copepod

Crab larva

FOOD SIEVE
Each comb-like gill raker is made of keratin, a material similar to human fingernails. Basking sharks shed their gill rakers in winter when the plankton supply diminishes, but grow new ones in the spring.

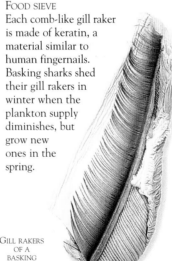

GILL RAKERS
OF A
BASKING
SHARK

81

Whale and megamouth shark

Whale and megamouth sharks are plankton eaters that live in tropical waters. Both are enormous in size: the whale shark is the largest of all fish and may grow to a length of 18 m (59 ft) and weigh up to 40 tonnes (44 tons). The megamouth measures more than 4 m (13 ft). Anatomically, the megamouth is more closely related to the great white than to other filter feeders.

Open mouth of the whale shark

OPEN WIDE
The whale shark's mouth is small compared to that of a basking shark. The gill arches are connected by gristly bars that support mesh filters which trap plankton.

TINY TEETH
Whale sharks have a large number of tiny teeth that serve no function as they cannot chew or tear food. However, divers can be bruised if an arm or leg becomes caught on the shark's teeth.

WHALE SHARK TEETH

ANCESTRAL BEHAVIOUR
Whale sharks have been observed more or less vertical in the water when feeding on small fish such as anchovies. This unusual feeding posture probably harks back to the habits of their ancient ancestors.

DIVER FRIENDLY

Whale sharks are placid animals that will tolerate divers holding on to their fins. They lay the world's largest eggs, which are at least 40 times as big as a chicken's egg. The embryos of whale sharks may grow to more than 35 cm (14 in) long.

Longer upper lobe of tail

Silvery luminescence round the mouth is thought to attract shrimps and other food

NEW SPECIES

The megamouth shark escaped the attention of science until 1976 when one was accidentally caught off the coast of Hawaii by a US research vessel. It was hauled aboard so scientists could examine the specimen in detail.

MEGAMOUTH SHARK

83

STRANGE SHARKS

SOME OF THE MOST UNUSUAL sharks live in rarely explored habitats. Some species are known by only one or two specimens, so their behaviour can only be guessed at. Sometimes there may be clues, such as the curious wounds in the bodies of seals and whales – which turned out to be the work of the cookiecutter shark.

ODD BITE

Cookiecutters are only 50 cm (20 in) long, yet they have the largest teeth, compared to their size, of any living shark. They feed by gouging round plugs of flesh from their victims.

Disc-shaped bite from cookiecutter

COOKIECUTTER

This dwarf shark is only about 15 cm (6 in) long

Flexible lips clamp onto prey

It is protected by a spine on its first dorsal fin

DWARF SHARK

The dwarf shark is known from very few specimens. It lives in deep water, in the Pacific Ocean. It seems likely that it makes vertical migrations, as it has also been caught in shallow seas. Like many deep-sea fish, it has light organs on its underside

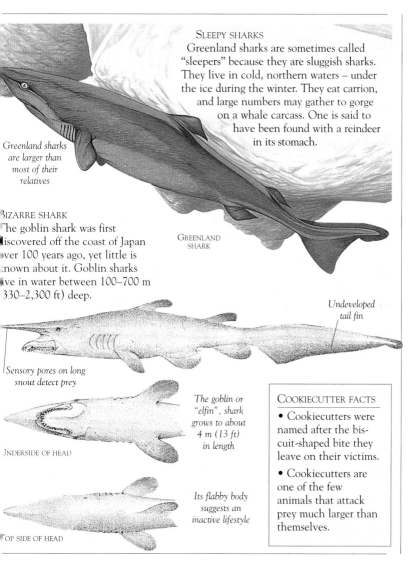

SLEEPY SHARKS

Greenland sharks are sometimes called "sleepers" because they are sluggish sharks. They live in cold, northern waters – under the ice during the winter. They eat carrion, and large numbers may gather to gorge on a whale carcass. One is said to have been found with a reindeer in its stomach.

Greenland sharks are larger than most of their relatives

GREENLAND SHARK

BIZARRE SHARK

The goblin shark was first discovered off the coast of Japan over 100 years ago, yet little is known about it. Goblin sharks live in water between 100–700 m (330–2,300 ft) deep.

Undeveloped tail fin

Sensory pores on long snout detect prey

UNDERSIDE OF HEAD

The goblin or "elfin", shark grows to about 4 m (13 ft) in length

TOP SIDE OF HEAD

Its flabby body suggests an inactive lifestyle

COOKIECUTTER FACTS

• Cookiecutters were named after the biscuit-shaped bite they leave on their victims.

• Cookiecutters are one of the few animals that attack prey much larger than themselves.

87

SHARK ODDITIES

SHARKS ARE SUPREME evolutionary opportunists, filling all kinds of roles and thriving in almost all marine habitats. Some even mimic the appearance – and success – of other fish, such as rays and sawfish, but beneath their sometimes strange surface appearance, the true structure of the shark remains.

STARRY RAY
Rays have cartilaginous skeletons and dermal denticles like sharks, but have followed a separate evolutionary path since the time of the dinosaurs. The starry ray lives on the seabed in cold waters round the coasts of Europe and eastern North America.

Equal-sized teeth

SAWFISH TEETH

SAWFISH
Sawfish are related to rays but have long, flattened snouts like sawsharks. Sawfish teeth are all the same size, whereas sawsharks have different sized teeth. Sawfish grow to more than 10 m (33 ft) in length.

Sawshark teeth are different sizes

SAWSHARK
Sawsharks stir up the seabed with their long, toothed snout, feeling for small fish and crabs with their barbels. Baby sawsharks' teeth are covered with skin up to the time they are born, so they don't injure their mother or each other.

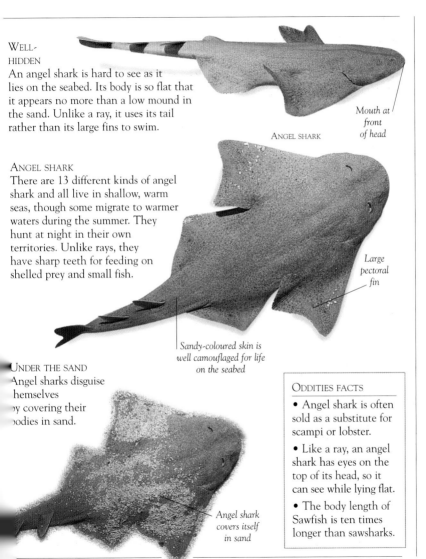

WELL-HIDDEN

An angel shark is hard to see as it lies on the seabed. Its body is so flat that it appears no more than a low mound in the sand. Unlike a ray, it uses its tail rather than its large fins to swim.

ANGEL SHARK

Mouth at front of head

ANGEL SHARK

There are 13 different kinds of angel shark and all live in shallow, warm seas, though some migrate to warmer waters during the summer. They hunt at night in their own territories. Unlike rays, they have sharp teeth for feeding on shelled prey and small fish.

Large pectoral fin

Sandy-coloured skin is well camouflaged for life on the seabed

UNDER THE SAND

Angel sharks disguise themselves by covering their bodies in sand.

Angel shark covers itself in sand

ODDITIES FACTS

• Angel shark is often sold as a substitute for scampi or lobster.

• Like a ray, an angel shark has eyes on the top of its head, so it can see while lying flat.

• The body length of Sawfish is ten times longer than sawsharks.

EVOLUTIONARY LEFTOVERS

TODAY'S SEAS provide an environment similar to that of the ancient oceans in which sharks evolved. Some sharks have become extinct, their places taken by more efficient species, but others have survived unchanged for millions of years. Several species were only known to science from fossils before the living animals were found.

SEVEN-GILLED SHARK
Some rare sharks have six, or even seven gill openings. The way the jaws are attached to the skull, and the fact that there is little calcium hardening their vertebrae makes them similar to primitive sharks.

SEVEN-GILLED SHARK

Grows to almost 2 m (7 ft) in length

Eel-like body shape

LIVING FOSSIL
More than any other shark, the frilled shark can be called a living fossil. It has six gill slits, the first of which is very long and looks like a frilly collar. It is almost eel-like in shape, and certain features of its vertebrae, its blood system, and its lateral line are no longer found in modern sharks.

FRILLED SHARK

HORN HABITS

The horn shark rests during the day, often in groups of several individuals. It hunts at night, using its sense of smell to find food. Though not closely related to the extinct *Hybodus*, it has large spines on the leading edge of its dorsal fins.

Short "bull face" of horn shark

HORN SHARK

HORN FOSSIL

The earliest fossil of a horn shark dates back about 150 million years. Today, similar sharks feed on shelled prey, which they crush with flat-topped teeth much like those of ancient fossils.

DEEP-SEA HUNTER

The frilled shark is armed with about 300 teeth, set in 27 rows. Each tooth carries three sharp hooks, so prey stand little chance of escape.

FRILLED SHARK TEETH

EVOLUTIONARY FACTS

• Frilled sharks are found in deep water throughout the world, but are not common anywhere.

• Horn sharks use fin spines to burrow under rocks, searching for prey, which are often worn down to half their length.

SHARKS FOR THE FUTURE

DIVERSITY IN THE SEA

SINCE ANCIENT TIMES, sharks have been part of almost every marine environment, but today many species are threatened. Many people ask why the oceans need dangerous creatures such as sharks, but being major predators, sharks play an important role in preserving the balance of nature in the sea.

ABUNDANT SPECIES
There are more kinds of catshark than any other group of sharks, yet most of them are unfamiliar. They are usually small, few measuring more than 1 m (3 ft) in length, and often live on the seabed.

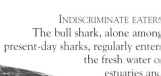

GULF CAT-
SHARK

INDISCRIMINATE EATER
The bull shark, alone among present-day sharks, regularly enters the fresh water of estuaries and rivers. It thus comes into regular contact with humans and can be dangerous. It will eat almost any flesh, fresh or carrion, and is also attracted to waste thrown into rivers.

TOP PREDATOR

Because humans fall within the size range of its usual food, the great white may attack bathers and surfers. As a result, it is more feared and hated than more common – and possibly more dangerous sharks.

The great white is an endangered species

DIVERSITY FACTS

• Between them, sharks are able to feed on almost all creatures found in the sea.

• Over 340 species of sharks are known, but there may be more deep-water species to be found.

GREAT WHITE SHARK

BIG FISH

The largest of all fish, the whale shark sifts plankton from the sea with its gill rakers. It also eats small fish, which may enable its worn gill rakers to regrow. It is possible that another plankton-feeder, the basking shark, hibernates to renew its gill rakers.

The whale shark has a smaller mouth than other plankton eaters

WHALE SHARK

SMALLEST SHARK

The Lantern shark is the smallest of all sharks. It has been recorded at depths of 2,000 m (6,600 ft). Finding food and a mate is difficult at these cold, dark depths, but its light organs may help with both vital activities. It is possible that it hunts in groups.

SOUTHERN LANTERN SHARK

DIVERSITY IN THE SEA

ENDANGERED SHARKS

SOME SPECIES of shark are rare because of over-exploitation by humans. All sharks breed slowly, some producing no more than two young a year, and many mature slowly, so that a depleted population cannot recover quickly.

LEFT TO DIE
Many sharks are seriously injured by game fishermen who hunt them for sport and leave them to die on the sea floor. Sometimes the fins are cut off a live shark to be sold. The body is then thrown back into the sea to die. In some parts of the West Indies and the Australian coast the seabed is littered with corpses.

ENDANGERED YOUNG
Female sharks are larger than males, which makes them sought after by trophy hunters. Some species, such as blue sharks, swim into inshore waters to give birth. For every female caught, a litter of young has been lost – something that no animal species can withstand for long.

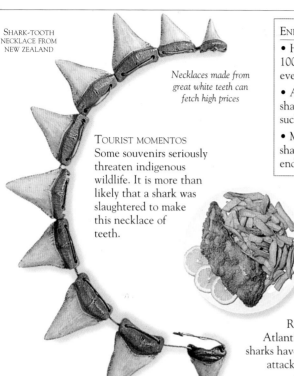

SHARK-TOOTH
NECKLACE FROM
NEW ZEALAND

*Necklaces made from
great white teeth can
fetch high prices*

TOURIST MOMENTOS

Some souvenirs seriously
threaten indigenous
wildlife. It is more than
likely that a shark was
slaughtered to make
this necklace of
teeth.

ENDANGERED FACTS

• Humans kill up to
100 million sharks
every year.

• As slow breeders,
sharks cannot replace
such losses.

• Many species of
shark are already
endangered.

*Because of overfishing,
sharks are now rare
where they were once
abundant*

UNDER ATTACK

The piked dogfish
is one of many
small sharks caught
each year for food.
Recently in the North
Atlantic, the larger oceanic
sharks have come under similar
attack and have drastically
declined in numbers.

PRICELESS JAWS

Despite their high price, shark jaws are
popular with tourists, who severely
endanger the shark population by
buying them. However, attitudes may
be changing: for example, a recent
study in the Maldives estimated that a
living grey reef shark could generate
US $2,500 in tourism. The same shark
dead would fetch only US $24.

INDUSTRY

THE KILLING OF SHARKS for industrial use has a long history, since almost half the known species of shark have some commercial value. In the past, sharks' teeth were used as weapons, their skin was used as sandpaper, and their livers for oil. Today they are still hunted, but numbers are now in serious decline.

HAMMERHEAD TRAPPED IN NET

FISHING NETS
Sharks can easily become trapped in fishing nets used by trawlers or safety nets used to protect bathing beaches. Once entangled, it is almost impossible for them to escape. They often end up drowning as they cannot keep water flowing over their gills.

ENVIRONMENTAL POLLUTION
Some sharks have been found with plastic packaging straps caught around their bodies. As the shark grows, the plastic gradually cuts into its flesh, resulting in horrific injuries to its body.

Because sharks cannot swim backwards, they are unable to free themselves from packing straps that become caught around their bodies

LIVER PILLS

Health pills made from shark's liver claim to reduce the incidence of heart disease and cancer, and to increase longevity. For many years, shark livers were used as a source of Vitamins A and E until a synthetic alternative was discovered in the 1950s.

Shark-fin fibres look like noodles

SHARK-FIN SOUP

ASIAN DELICACY

Shark-fin soup is made from the cartilaginous fibres in the fin of a shark. After the fins are cut from the shark and hung to dry, they are soaked and repeatedly boiled to extract the fibres. Other ingredients are added to the soup to give it flavour.

Plastic that has cut into the shark's body

Tiger, dusky, and bull sharks have been found off the coast of Florida badly injured by plastic straps

COSMETICS

The gall bladder and part of the shark's liver have been shown to improve acne and other skin complaints. However, natural plant oils are just as effective for improving these skin conditions.

INDUSTRY FACTS

• As it becomes more affordable, shark-fin soup is increasing in popularity throughout the world.

• Drift nets used to catch squid in the North Pacific also catch about 1.8 million blue sharks each year.

99

TOURISM

ECOTOURISM, one of the fastest-growing tourism markets, could well be the key to some sharks' long-term survival. Sharks, swimming free in their own habitat, offer enormous economic potential as a tourist attraction.

SHARK PHOTOGRAPHY

Professional shark photographers often work from the protection of an underwater cage, particularly when filming a dangerous shark such as the great white. As a service for tourists, underwater safaris could give amateurs similar shelter and excitement.

Tail fluke of sperm whale off the coast of New Zealand

WHALE APPEAL

Whale watching is a valuable part of ecotourism. In some countries, it is now a bigger industry than hunting ever was. It is possible that shark watching trips may also become a tourist attraction. Sharks are easily attracted using bait and unlike whales are less likely to be upset or distressed by the presence of humans.

IN THE RING

There are places where shark wrestling is staged as an attraction for tourists. While it apparently does little damage to the shark, it is one of the least desirable activities concerning tourism and sharks.

SHARK DIVES

Swimming with sharks is an exciting experience for the adventurous. Specialist tour operators can organize dives with hammerhead, reef, whale, and blue sharks – even the great white (which must be viewed from the safety of a strong cage).

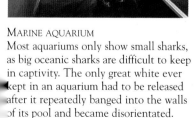

MARINE AQUARIUM

Most aquariums only show small sharks, as big oceanic sharks are difficult to keep in captivity. The only great white ever kept in an aquarium had to be released after it repeatedly banged into the walls of its pool and became disorientated.

SHARKS IN SCIENCE

IN LABORATORIES in many parts of the world, teams of scientists are grappling with the intricacies of shark life, anatomy, and biochemistry. Much research centres on the fact that sharks appear to be unusually disease-free. The shark's physiological secrets may prove of great benefit to humankind.

DENTICLE RESEARCH

In the past, a shark's dermal denticles have provided information about teeth and their formation. More recently, scientists have come to believe that a shark's denticles move to affect water flow over its body. This may have potential applications in the field of ship and aircraft design.

DENTICLES
X 110 MAGNIFICATION

Ridges on the denticles help to reduce drag

MONEY-SAVER

Tiny grooves on the dermal denticles of sharks such as hammerheads can reduce drag by up to ten per cent. Scientists are studying how these grooves work as a reduction in drag of only one or two per cent could save the airline industry billions of dollars in fuel costs, as well as helping engineers design safer planes.

ANTIBIOTIC BREAKTHROUGH

Shark liver is a rich source of a steroid called squalamine. Its chief value seems to be as an antibiotic that may protect patients against bacteria, fungi, and other disease-causing organisms. It could also be useful in attacking bacteria that have become resistant to other drugs.

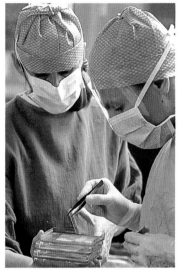

ARTIFICIAL SKIN

Here, in a medical laboratory, artificial skin grown from shark-fin cartilage is being used as a graft to heal a serious burn. Squalamine will increase its chance of success.

CURE FOR DISEASE

Besides being caught for food in large numbers, the spiny dogfish has contributed to our understanding of salt removal from the bloodstream. The mechanism that it employs to do this is proving useful as a way of treating the disease cystic fibrosis.

SPINY DOGFISH

SCIENCE FACTS

• Shark gall bladders have been used in the treatment of acne.

• Liver oil is still used in some cosmetics.

• Corneas from the eyes of sharks are used in some human transplant operations.

RESEARCH

ALTHOUGH HUMANS have had contact with sharks since prehistoric times, most research into their behaviour is comparatively recent. Work with living sharks is mainly concerned with lifespan and migrations; it usually involves tagging or radio tracking individuals for a short time.

TAGGING SHARKS

Baited hooks are used to catch a shark

The shark is carefully brought on board

REELING IN
A shark must be caught before it can be tagged. Most tagging is done by game fishermen who record the weight and size of the shark on special cards issued by research institutions.

TAGGING
The tag, which is a non-corrosive numbered disc or dart, is placed securely in the muscles just below the first dorsal fin. Should the shark be caught again in another part of the world, there is an address on the reverse side of the tag where it can be returned.

RELEASE
Once tagged, the shark is returned to the sea. If it is caught again, the catcher should inform the tagging authority so that information about the shark can be recorded and exchanged.

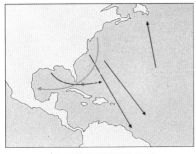

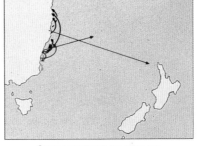

ATLANTIC SHARK MOVEMENTS

SHARK MOVEMENTS OFF AUSTRALIA

OCEAN MOVEMENTS

Few sharks are recovered, but some are known to have
lived for as long as 20 years after they were tagged. These
maps show shark movements tracked as a result of tagging
on the east coasts of the US and Australia. Apart from
the Port Jackson shark, the species tagged are fairly large
and active. Small and deep-water sharks do not feature in
these studies as they are hard to catch and follow.

SHARK KEY
WHALER: BLACK
HAMMERHEAD: LIGHT BLUE
SANDBAR: GREEN
TIGER: YELLOW
PORT JACKSON: RED
MAKO: DARK BLUE

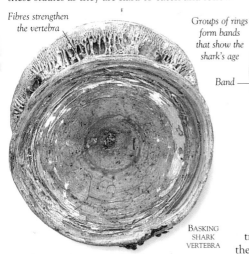

*Fibres strengthen
the vertebra*

*Groups of rings
form bands
that show the
shark's age*

Band

BASKING
SHARK
VERTEBRA

AGE RINGS

Sharks continue to grow
throughout their lives, usually
with seasonal spurts of growth.
Scientists can assess the age
and growth rates of sharks by
treating the bones (vertebrae) of
their backs with special chemicals.

PROTECTION

THE LARGE-SCALE destruction of sharks, mainly in the second half of this century, has led ecologists to pressure governments to protect both it and its environment. Despite opposition in some quarters, the killing of sharks is now controlled in many parts of the world.

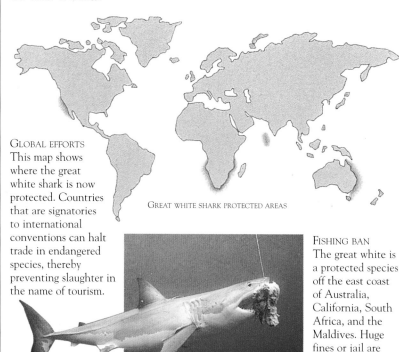

GLOBAL EFFORTS
This map shows where the great white shark is now protected. Countries that are signatories to international conventions can halt trade in endangered species, thereby preventing slaughter in the name of tourism.

GREAT WHITE SHARK PROTECTED AREAS

FISHING BAN
The great white is a protected species off the east coast of Australia, California, South Africa, and the Maldives. Huge fines or jail are the penalty for breaking the ban.

EXTINCT SPECIES

Hybodus was a common shark alive during the time of the dinosaurs, yet about 65 million years ago, it became extinct. However, *Hybodus* disappeared gradually as modern sharks evolved. Today, wanton killing of sharks by humans leaves no time for replacement.

Hybodus had a large spine in front of both its dorsal fins

PROTECTION FACTS

• Spiny dogfish must survive 20 years before they can breed.

• The great white shark was protected in South Africa in 1991, and in California, US, and Tasmania, Australia in 1994.

ACHILL ISLAND FISHERY STATISTICS

The table shows the decline in the numbers of basking shark caught off the Irish coast over a 20-year period. Fifty years ago the sight of a large school was commonplace. Now, owing to drastic over-exploitation it is no longer. The basking shark is a protected species round the British coast.

YEAR	NUMBER OF SHARKS TAKEN	TONNES (TONS) OF OIL SOLD
1951	1,630	340 (375)
1953	1,068	209 (230)
1955	1,708	122 (135)
1957	468	94 (104)
1959	280	64 (70)
1961	258	54 (59)
1963	75	17 (19)
1965	47	11 (12)
1967	41	10 (11)
1969	113	26 (29)
1971	29	6 (7)
1973	85	17 (19)
1975	38	8 (9)

PROTECTED SPECIES

After the late 1940s, when basking sharks were killed by harpoons with explosive heads, numbers declined drastically. Basking sharks are slow breeders and though they are now protected, it will be a long time before large numbers build up again.

107

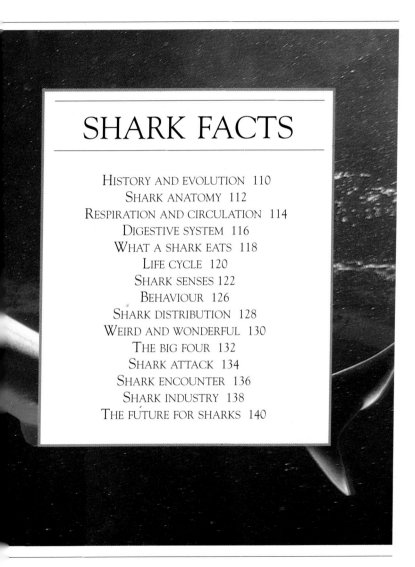

SHARK FACTS

HISTORY AND EVOLUTION

PREHISTORIC SHARKS

The first sharks appeared in the oceans around 450 million years ago, long before the dinosaurs roamed the Earth.

- Thelodonts are a branch of the shark family that are now extinct.

- *Xenacanth* was a freshwater shark.

- *Cladoselache* appeared 400 million years ago. Unlike modern sharks, its mouth was at the tip of its snout.

- Some ancient sharks were eaten by Arthrodires, armoured fish that measured over 6 m (19.5 ft) in length.

- *Carcharadon megalodon* appeared 10-25 million years ago. These massive fish measured over 12 m (40 ft) in length.

- Many fossil *megalodon* teeth have been discovered. Their teeth were at least twice the size of a modern-day great white's.

- Some people believe that some examples of *megalodon* may still exist in the world's deepest oceans.

SHARK SPECIES

There are several hundred different species of shark. These are the species names of some of the best known sharks.

- Carchariniformes are also known as groundsharks. The tiger shark is part of this group.

- Orectolobiformes, or carpet sharks, include wobbegong and whale sharks.

- Squaliformes are known as dogfish.

- The shark family of squatiniformes are also known as angel sharks.

- Heterodontiformes are sometimes called bullhead sharks, a group that includes the Port Jackson shark.

- Lamniformes are called mackerel sharks. Makos, great whites, threshers, goblins, megamouths, and porbeagle sharks are all members of this group.

ANCIENT SHARK

This is a reconstruction of *Cladoselache*, one of the earliest known sharks. It measured around 2 m (6.6 ft) long and had a powerful tail, which probably allowed it to swim very fast.

SHARK RELATIVES

- Sharks are members of the elasmobranch family of fish.

- All elasmobranchs have skeletons made of cartilage, not bone.

- Rays and chimeras are also part of the elasmobranch family.

- Stingrays are armed with one, or sometimes several venomous spines on their tales.

- Manta rays, or devil rays, can weigh up to 1,400 kg (3,087 lb).

- Guitarfish – a type of ray – spend most of the time buried in the sand.

- Chimeras, also known as ratfish, have a clasper (reproductive organ) on their foreheads.

Although they look very different, rays are closely related to sharks.

MYTHS AND BELIEFS

- Some people believe that the "greate fyshe" that swallowed Jonah in the biblical tale was a reference to a shark, rather than a whale.

- The Australian Aborigines have revered the shark as a great source of oil and meat for centuries.

- The Maoris of New Zealand used to hunt dog shark in a ritual overseen by priests on certain days of the year.

- The Braamen – shark charmers in Sri Lanka – cast spells to prevent pearl fishermen from being eaten.

- In parts of Africa, boatbuilders sometimes anoint the wood of a new vessel with hammerhead oil to bring good winds and a successful voyage.

- On some Pacific islands, sharks were thought of as gods. As such, they were never eaten.

SHARKS vs BONY FISH

- A shark's skeleton is made of cartilage. Most other types of fish have skeletons of bone.

- Bony fish have swim bladders to aid buoyancy. A shark has a large, oil-rich liver to keep it buoyant.

- A shark has an asymmetrical, or hypercercal, tail which helps to keep it from sinking.

- A bony fish's skin is covered in smooth scales; a shark's is made up of rough denticles.

- Bony fish have a gill cover, or operculum, rather than gill slits.

- Some sharks have dark muscle, this allows them to be warmer than their surroundings. This means they are warm-blooded.

- All bony fish are cold-blooded.

The denticles covering a shark's skin give it a very rough feel if stroked the "wrong" way.

BODY PARASITES AND HELPERS

- Copepods attach themselves to a shark's fins and gills.

- There are over a thousand copepods that parasitise sharks.

- Copepods feed off skin secretions and blood.

- Remoras have a suction pad on their heads.

- Remoras or sucker fish attach themselves to a shark's skin.

- A shark's gut can contain hundreds of tapeworms.

- Cleaner fish remove parasites from a sharks teeth and gills.

- Banded coral shrimp eat the parasites found on a shark's skin.

- Marine leeches live around a shark's cloaca or claspers.

- Roundworms and flatworms also use sharks as their host.

SHARK FACTS

- Dorsal – positioned on the shark's back. Some types of shark have two, with an additional, smaller fin close to the tail.

- Dorsal spines – only present in the primitive dogfish and heterodonts.

- Pectoral – paired fins close to the gill slits that allow the shark to control its direction.

- Pelvic – paired fins underneath the shark that aid stability. The claspers are positioned on the inner edge of the pelvic fins.

- Anal – single fin positioned on the underside of the shark.

- Caudal fin – the tail. There are many different shapes and sizes of caudal fins throughout the shark world.

INTERNAL ANATOMY

A shark's internal anatomy is similar to that of most vertebrate animals. The heart pumps blood around the body, delivering oxygen and nutrients while taking away carbon dioxide and other wastes. Food is digested in the stomach and passes into the large, tube-like intestine where the digested food is absorbed. Kidneys remove wastes from the blood. The body wall has powerful muscles for swimming while the cartilage skeleton provides support. The brain passes signals along the spinal cord.

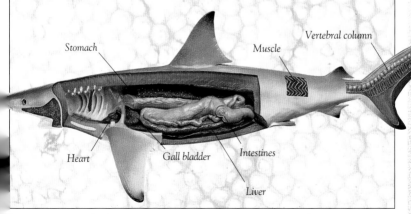

Stomach

Muscle

Vertebral column

Heart

Gall bladder

Intestines

Liver

RESPIRATION AND CIRCULATION

BREATHING

- Sharks, like all fish, breathe by extracting oxygen dissolved in the water. As they do so, carbon dioxide is passed back into the water.

- The water passes into a shark's mouth and is forced over the gills. It was once thought that sharks had to keep swimming to do this, but it is now known that some sharks can pump water over their gills while remaining stationary.

- Fast-moving sharks, such as mackerel sharks, use ram-jet ventilation to breathe – the water is forced over their gills as they move along quickly.

- Slower movers, such as wobbegongs, pump the water across the gills by closing their mouths and and contracting the mouth and gullet walls.

- The grey nurse shark uses both systems – ram-jet while swimming and respiratory pumping while on the sea bottom.

Grey nurse sharks conserve energy by using the respiratory pumping method to breathe.

HOW GILLS WORK

- Gills are arch-shaped and made of cartilage. Fine, feathered filaments lie across the gill arches.

- Each filament is made up of thousands of tiny, leaflike branches called lamellae. This creates a very large surface area, designed to absorb as much oxygen as possible.

- The lamellae contain very tiny blood vessels called capillaries.

- Blood flowing around the capillaries is very close to the water outside. Oxygen in the water is absorbed into the blood through the capillaries, while carbon dioxide passes out in the opposite direction.

BLOOD AND OXYGEN

- Haemoglobin is the chemical that carries oxygen in the blood. When haemoglobin absorbs oxygen, it turns red, giving blood its colour.

- The haemoglobin count is a way of showing how efficient a blood type is at carrying oxygen.

- Whaler sharks have low haemoglobin counts, so their blood is not good at oxygen transport.

- Benthic sharks (bottom dwellers) have even lower haemoglobin counts.

- Mackerel sharks have relatively high counts, so their blood transports oxygen well.

CIRCULATORY SYSTEM

- Sharks have a heart with four chambers, just like mammals.

- Blood collects in the first chamber and is pumped through the second and third. The fourth chamber prevents blood from flowing back into the heart.

- Fast-moving sharks, such as the Mako shark, have bigger hearts than those that move slowly, such as wobbegong sharks.

- A larger heart allows the shark to pump blood around the body more quickly, allowing its body functions to be carried out faster.

BREATHING SLITS

Most sharks have five gill slits on each side of the head; some have up to seven. Some bottom-dwellers draw in water through a spiracle – an additional, rounded gill opening on the top of their heads.

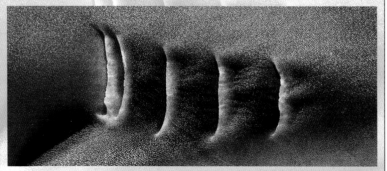

DIGESTIVE SYSTEM

JAWS AND TEETH

- A shark's jaws are separate from its skull. They are attached to it by flexible ligaments and muscles.

- A predatory shark, such as the great white, tilts its head back and pushes both of its jaws forward as it opens its mouth.

- Once a shark takes hold of its prey it uses a sawing motion to rip lumps off.

- The pressure exerted by a large shark's bite can reach 60 kg (132 lb) per tooth.

- Filter-feeders, such as the whale shark, have hundreds of tiny teeth arranged in rows to form a rasping, sandpaper-like arrangement.

- Great whites have triangular teeth with serrated edges.

- Nurse sharks have flat, slablike teeth for crushing shellfish.

- Heterodonts, such as the Port Jackson shark, have small, sharp teeth at the front to catch prey and big molars behind them to crush it.

- Cookiecutters have been known to bite chunks out of submarines.

STOMACH

- A shark's stomach is very flexible and is able to expand to hold a large meal.

- It is filled with powerful digestive juices that break down food.

- A shark's stomach is not round but U-shaped.

- Few sharks ever have a full stomach.

- The stomach pushes itself out to regurgitate indigestible objects.

- The mackerel shark's raised body temperature allows it to digest food more quickly than other sharks.

NEW TEETH

Sharks' teeth are arranged in rows and are constantly being replaced. The process of tooth replacement begins even as the shark is developing in the egg case or mother shark.

A shark may get through as many as 20,000 teeth in its lifetime.

FOOD REQUIREMENTS

- Most sharks are cold-blooded and need less food than warm-blooded creatures.

- Warm-blooded sharks need to eat 2 kg (4.5 lb) of food per day.

- A typical shark consumes around 0.5 to 3% of of its body weight per day.

- Most sharks eat once every two or three days.

- One meal can keep a great white going for two months.

- Food reserves can be stored in a shark's large liver.

Young lemon sharks need about 20,000 calories a day to maintain their body weight.

DIGESTION AND THE SPIRAL VALVE

- The shark has little room in its body for its intestines.

- Most of the space inside a shark's body is taken up by the liver, stomach, and reproductive organs.

- The corkscrew-shaped spiral valve – the shark's intestine – is designed to create as large a surface area as possible.

- The spiral-valve intestine allows the food to be digested in a small space.

- The gall bladder releases bile into the intestines to aid digestion.

- The excellent efficiency of the intestines enables the shark to eat a small amount of food relative to its size.

- The spiral valve slows up digestion, and it may take four days to digest one meal.

- The remnants of the meal pass out through the cloaca.

WHAT A SHARK EATS

SHARK TASTES

- Heterodonts eat mostly echinoderms – sea urchins for example.

- Gummy sharks prefer to eat crustacea – crabs and lobsters.

- Pelagic whalers eat squid and fish.

- Weasel sharks eat mostly octopus.

- Great whites eat marine mammals and turtles.

- Young mako sharks like to eat octopus and squid.

- Mature mako sharks eat marlin and swordfish.

- Most sharks and rays eat meat. The large, slow-moving filter-feeders, such as the whale and basking sharks, eat plankton and algae.

- The tiger shark is regarded as omnivorous – it will eat anything.

- The cookiecutter is effectively a parasite, taking small chunks of flesh out of large sea creatures.

PREDATORS

- Most sharks will not attack healthy animals that can escape easily.

- Sharks prefer to go for injured, diseased, or dying creatures – those that cannot fight back. This is an easy way to get a meal.

- Great whites can often be seen attacking dead whales.

- Tiger sharks have been known to pull seabirds from the surface.

- Apart from man, a shark's biggest enemy is a bigger shark.

- The hammerhead shark hunts and eats stingrays. It swallows them whole, apparently unaffected by the stingray's poisonous spine.

CANNIBAL SHARKS

Most sharks will eat any other shark, including their own kind. Leopard sharks, such as the one shown here, are eaten by young great whites off the Pacific Coast of North America.

NOT JUST MEAT

- Whale and basking sharks do not eat meat. These sharks eat plankton, microscopic organisms in the water.

- As plankton eaters swim, they keep their mouths open to pass water through their gills.

- Gill rakers are like a comb found on the gills. The rakers sieve out the food from the water.

- The filtering process is aided by sticky slime or mucus that coats the gills.

- Basking sharks shed these rakers during winter, when food is less plentiful, and grow new ones for the new season.

- Plankton is found in the surface layers of the sea, so this is where these sharks spend most of their time.

Seawater analyzed under a microscope shows it to be teeming with plankton.

MANEATERS

- Sharks have been known to attack humans for a number of reasons.

- The most common reason is that they have provoked a shark.

- Attacks are provoked by spearfishing in shark-infested waters, or hurting or threatening the shark.

- Someone paddling on a surfboard looks like a sea lion seen from below.

- Great whites sometimes mistake people for sea lions and attack them.

- Someone on a boogie board – a circular type of surfboard – looks like a turtle in the water to a shark.

LIFE CYCLE

MATING

- All sharks undergo internal fertilization.

- The male uses one of two claspers to introduce sperm to the female's egg tube, or oviduct.

- Two muscular sacs in the belly of the shark fill with seawater and this is squirted along the clasper to flush the sperm into the oviduct.

- The females may retain the sperm until the next season to fertilize their eggs.

- In smaller, flexible species the male coils around the female and holds on with its jaws.

- In larger species, the mating pair lie in a parallel, head-to-head position.

MERMAIDS' PURSES

The embryos of dogfish and rays develop inside egg cases. Once the young have hatched, these empty egg cases are discarded and wash ashore. They have been called mermaids' purses because of their shape.

REPRODUCTION

- There are three different reproduction methods found in the shark world. They are called viviparous, oviparous, and ovoviviparous.

- Viviparous means the young are born fully formed.

- The lemon shark (viviparous) gives birth to live young that are nourished by a placenta, much like the other vertebrate creatures.

- Ovoviviparous means they produce eggs that hatch within the body.

- Tiger sharks (ovoviviparous) develop in their membrane-encased eggs.

- Oviparous means egg laying.

- Sharks' eggs are called mermaids' purses.

- The bullhead, swellhead, and catsharks are all egg-layers (oviparous).

- Oophagy (interuterine cannibalism) exists in threshers, makos, and porbeagles, where the female continues to ovulate and the developing sharks use these eggs as a food source.

- In grey nurse sharks, the first pup to develop actually eats all its siblings as they hatch.

GROWTH AND DEVELOPMENT

- Sharks grow slowly due to their slow digestion and feeding rates.

- In its first year, a lemon shark needs to eat six times its own weight in order to double its size.

- Lemon sharks reach maturity at 15 years.

- The fastest growers are large pelagic sharks, such as the blue shark. It can grow at a rate of 30 cm (12 in) a year.

- Sharks grow fastest in their early years, and slow as they age.

- Growth rates of captive sharks can be 10 times their normal rate.

LIFESPAN

Scientists have found it difficult to establish the maximum ages of sharks. It is thought that most types live for 20 to 30 years. However, some sharks appear to grow to be very old. The piked dogfish matures at 20 and is thought to live for up to 80 years. Some people have even suggested that a great white shark can live to be 100 years old. Other people believe that the large, slow-moving whale shark may live to be even older, possibly even reaching an age of 150 years! If this is true, then the whale shark would be one of the longest-living creatures on the planet.

The star-spotted smooth hound has the shortest lifespan of any shark – it lives for only 10 years.

121

SHARK FACTS

EYES

- The structure of a shark's eye is basically the same as all other vertebrates.

- Light receptors in the retina, called rods, detect black and white; cones detect colour.

- Sharks have a lot of rods compared to cones in their retina, so it is thought that they cannot pick out colourful details. However, it means they are very able to detect moving objects in dim light.

- Sharks that live in shallow waters, where it is fairly light, tend to have small eyes.

- Those that inhabit deep waters have larger eyes, probably to make the most of the little amount of light that is available.

- Some sharks have a special membrane that protects the eye from any damage that might be caused by thrashing prey when the shark is feeding.

- A great white simply rolls its eye back to do this.

SMELL

- A shark has its nostrils located in front of its eyes, either side of the snout.

- As a shark swims, water flows through its nostrils.

- Olfactory sacs in the nostrils detect scent in the water.

- Sharks respond strongly to the scent of body fluids and secretions of injured or distressed animals.

- It is thought that sharks can detect a scent from over a mile away.

- Blacktips can detect one part of scent in 10 billion parts of water.

The epaulette shark has especially large nostrils for its size. Along with its barbels, these allow the shark to hunt out prey on the seabed.

EXTRA SENSORS

The pair of feelers, or barbels, on the nurse shark's nose allows it to feel for prey such as shrimps buried in the sand. It is thought that these barbels may also play a role in tasting and smelling food. Other sharks that live on the seabed have similar sensory organs.

EARS

- A shark's ear has all the structures found in other vertebrates. The ears are concerned with hearing and balance.

- A shark's ear openings are located on the top of its head.

- Sharks detect vibrations of water molecules as sound.

- Their ears can detect very low frequency sounds (25-100 hz).

- In certain parts of the ear, otoliths – calcium carbonate granules – tell the shark its angle of tilt in the water.

- Another part of the ear, the macula neglecta, tells the shark about its vertical movement.

TASTE

- The sense of taste is the least developed sense in sharks.

- A shark's tongue is supported by a pad of cartilage.

- Taste receptors are in the mouth and throat.

- The receptors contain sensory cells, similar to the olfactory sacs in the shark's nose.

- Sharks sometimes take a lump out of their prey in order to taste it.

- Some sharks mouth, or half-bite, to get a taste of their victim.

- After taking a bite, sharks may spit out their food if they don't like it.

BRAIN

- It used to be thought that sharks were brainless killers.

- Brain size and complexity varies from shark to shark.

- Brain to weight ratios suggest that sharks are "smarter" than bony fish.

- Large portions of the brain are dedicated to the sense of smell.

- Nurse sharks in captivity have been trained to press buttons with their snouts. Captive lemon sharks have been trained to distinguish between shapes and colours.

- Larger, active sharks have bigger brains than slow-moving bottom dwellers.

- Hammerheads have the largest brains in the shark world.

LORENZINI

- All organisms emit electrical signals that vary in strength depending on the animal.

- The shark's ampullae of Lorenzini allow it to detect electrical charges.

- This sense allows a shark to locate a fish buried in the sand.

- Sharks can detect their prey at close range using only this electric sense.

- The ampullae are delicate, jelly-filled canals connected to pores in the shark's skin.

- You can see pores for the ampullae on a shark's snout.

- Sharks can detect electrical fields of one hundred-millionth of a volt.

- It has been suggested that these ampullae also act like an built-in compass.

COMPASS SENSE

Some sharks migrate hundreds of kilometres and they seem to know where they are going. Scientists think that the ampullae of Lorenzini allow the sharks to "tune in" to the Earth's magnetic field, acting as kind of natural compass.

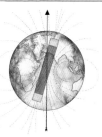

Sharks may be able to detect the Earth's magnetic field, allowing them to navigate over long distances.

LATERAL SENSE LINE

- The lateral line is a detection system which tells the shark about the movement and proximity of objects in the water.

- It is made up of specialized hair receptor cells found in grooves or canals along a central line which runs down either side of a shark's body and around the head.

- Water movement causes these hairs to bend and send signals to the brain.

- These receptors are used to detect the direction and amount of movement in the water.

- A shark can block off these receptors when it is feeding.

Model of a spinner shark showing the lateral line.

SENSING PREY

- Sharks usually pick up the smell of a victim first.

- The shark homes in on the bleeding prey.

- The lateral sense line confirms the position of the target.

- Sporadic electrical activity caused by the prey's muscles is picked up by the ampullae of Lorenzini.

- Closer in, the ears detect low level noises of the prey thrashing about.

- Now within striking distance, the shark can see the prey.

- The high amount of stimulation caused by the shark's senses makes the brain shut these senses down so that it is not distracted.

- The shark tastes the victim by biting it, then swims away.

- Once the shark has decided it likes the taste and the victim is moving less, it moves in for the kill.

BEHAVIOUR

BEHAVIOUR PATTERNS

- A shark's swimming motion is usually casual and deliberate.

- A shark will rarely make any sudden movements.

- A swell shark, when threatened, inhales water, doubling its size, so that it cannot be pulled from its sleeping place in the rocks.

- A shark's normal behaviour is such that other fish will ignore it.

- The noise made by humans usually scares sharks away.

- Curiosity often draws sharks towards scuba divers.

- Some sharks have been observed with divers being fed by hand and even stroked.

- Some sharks have learned where to find a large number of prey at certain times of the year.

POOL HUNTER

Epaulette sharks live on coral reefs in the southwest Pacific Ocean. They can crawl out of the water using their pectoral fins and move between rock pools, searching for small fish, crabs, shrimp, and other small creatures to eat.

TERRITORIAL SHARKS

- Most sharks are not territorial and simply swim around the sea.

- Reef sharks form a base and patrol it.

- Grey reef sharks may consider other sharks and people as a threat.

- Threat postures include arching the back and raising their snout.

- In breeding areas, mothers become very aggressive and territorial.

- White tip reef sharks stay in the same area for months, or even years.

- However, white tips are not known to aggressively defend their territory.

HUNTING

- The movements of a shark become erratic during hunting.

- Blue sharks become fearless, often attacking prey much bigger than themselves.

- Hammerheads will swim over the same area several times in order to home in on their prey.

- Great whites are known to patrol beaches that are home to populations of seals and sea lions.

ATTACK

- Sharks usually circle their prey before attacking it.

- They slowly narrow the circle, getting closer and closer.

- Grey reef sharks often nudge or bump the prey to see if it is soft.

- Great whites attack from below and behind, away from the head.

- South African great whites bite their prey in half.

- When there is a large amount of food, a feeding frenzy involving many sharks may occur.

- During the feeding frenzy, the sharks bite anything, including each other.

SOCIAL ANIMAL?

The great white shark used to be considered a loner. However, recent observations of this rarely-seen shark have shown that it may often live in pairs, sometimes with another of the same sex. Pairs have been observed hunting together and have also been known to migrate to the exact same spot, year after year.

127

FROM TOP TO BOTTOM

- The aggressive tiger shark spends most of its time close to the surface.

- Bonnetheads live close to the seabed in coastal waters.

- Greater hammerheads live in the deep ocean, but sometimes come into inland shallow waters.

- Makos can be found from the surface to the ocean depths.

- The rarely-seen megamouth lives in the mid-water region (half-way down) of the oceans.

- Saw sharks are always found on the bottom of the sea in shallow or deep waters.

- Sixgill sharks are found near the bottom of the sea.

- The catsharks all inhabit the bottom of the deepest seas.

The massive whale shark is found close to the surface, where it feeds on plankton.

GREAT TRAVELLERS

- The cookiecutter travels from the sea bottom to the surface to feed, a round-trip of up to 7 km (4.5 miles).

- Bull sharks do not limit themselves to the sea. They have been found 3,700 km (2,300 miles) up the Amazon river.

- The Ganges shark is also known to travel into freshwater.

- Atlantic blue sharks migrate the length and breadth of that ocean each year.

- Atlantic blues follow the Gulf Stream from the Caribbean to Europe, south along the coast of Africa and then back to the Caribbean – a round-trip of over 25,000 km (15,000 miles).

- The Greenland Shark lives in the Arctic Ocean.

- Salmon Sharks live in the Bering Sea.

- Porbeagles live in sub-Arctic waters.

- Oceanic white tips live in temperate and tropical waters.

- Whale sharks live in tropical waters.

- Bonnetheads and hammerheads live in the tropical regions of the southern hemisphere.

- Tiger sharks can be found as far south as New Zealand.

- Basking sharks can be found off the southern tips of Africa, South America, and New Zealand.

REEF SHARKS

- Black tips like the shallow waters of the back reef (coastal side).

- White tips like the steep vertical edges of some reef areas. They are often found sleeping in groups on ledges and in crevices.

- Grey reef sharks prefer the deeper waters of the fore reef (seaward side).

- Silvertips patrol the fore reef.

- Bull sharks and hammerheads are found further down the reef slope.

- The largest shark on a reef is the tiger. It can be found anywhere on the reef.

- The Galapagos shark is found only next to small island groups and never ventures far from land.

The black tip reef shark is found in the shallow parts of a reef, close to the shore.

WEIRD AND WONDERFUL

NAMES

- The sand tiger is known as the grey nurse in Australia and as the spotted raggedtooth in South Africa.

- Zebra sharks have spots.

- Megamouth sharks have a luminous mouth and more than one hundred rows of teeth.

- Mako is also the name of a small, fruit-bearing tree in New Zealand.

- Blind sharks close their eyes when they are taken out of the water.

- Great whites are also known as the white pointer and white death.

- Heterodont means "different tooth types".

- The timid shark is not dangerous to humans.

- Fishermen thought dogfish had teeth like a dog's, hence the name.

- Horn sharks get their name from the two horn-like spines on their backs next to each dorsal fin.

SPECIAL SHAPES

- Hammerheads use their flattened heads as "wings" to help them dive, rise, and turn.

- Hammerheads also use their heads to detect prey.

- Angel sharks are flattened like rays. Their bodies are the densest of all sharks and they live on the seabed.

- Frilled sharks are eel-like and can slip between the rocks on the seabed.

- A frilled shark's jaws can protrude like a snake's.

- The goblin shark has a very long snout, like a peaked cap.

The angel shark is so-called because of its extra-large pectoral fins that resemble an angel's wings.

RECORD HOLDERS

- The smallest shark is the dwarf shark, at only 10 cm (4 in) long.

- The piked dogfish is the most common shark in the world.

- The rarest shark is probably the megamouth. Only six specimens have ever been found.

- The most dangerous to humans are the bull, tiger, and great white sharks.

- The fastest swimmer is the mako shark, which can reach speeds of 32 kph (19 mph) for short periods.

- The largest shark caught by rod and line was a great white that weighed 1,200 kg (2,600 lb).

- An Australian tope shark tagged in 1951 was recaptured in 1986, only 214 km (130 miles) from its original release site.

- The deepest-diving sharks have been found at a depth of 3,500 m (11,500 ft), but they can go deeper.

- The greatest traveller is the blue shark, which migrates a distance of up to 3,000 km (1,875 miles).

- The least-travelled shark is the nurse shark, which stays in a small section of reef throughout its life.

MONSTERS AND GIANTS

- The largest shark is the whale shark. It measures up to 18 m (60 ft).

- The largest sharks known to attack humans are the great whites. They can grow to a length of up to 9 m (30 ft).

- The megamouth shark was only discovered in 1976. Measuring about 5 m (15 feet) long, it had a 1-m (3-ft) grin.

- Whale sharks are often run into by ships.

- It is thought that whale sharks may lay enormous eggs which measure up to 30 cm (12 in) in length.

- Basking sharks can measure up to 12 m (40 feet) in length and weigh over 4 tonnes (3.9 tons).

- *Carcharodon Megalodon*, an ancestor of the great white, is thought to have had a mouth 2 m (6 ft) across. In comparison, the largest set of jaws from a great white shark are only 57.5 cm (22.5 in) wide.

- Megalodon grew to a length of 13 m (43 ft) and had teeth that were more than twice as big as those of a great white shark.

WEIRD AND WONDERFUL

131

THE BIG FOUR

GREAT WHITES

- One of the "mackerel" sharks.

- The Mako and Porbeagle sharks are closely related to the great white.

- It has the scientific name *Carcharadon carcharinas*.

- The great white is greyish-brown or blue on its dorsal surface (back) and white or off-white on its ventral surface.

- It usually has a black spot at the the base of the pectoral fin.

- Up to 6 m (20 ft) in length, it is the largest of the predatory sharks.

- It is found in open oceans, estuaries, tropical and temperate waters.

- Great whites cruise slowly until stimulated by the presence of prey.

- Many attacks on humans are attributed to the great white.

The great white is one of the best known (and most feared) of all sharks.

MAKO

- The mako is a fast swimmer with similar characteristics to tuna.

- Its scientific name is *Isurus oxyrhinchus*.

- It is also known as the sharp-nosed mackerel, blue pointer, or bonito.

- It is blue or blueish-grey on the dorsal side and white on the ventral side.

- It lives mainly in the open ocean but comes close to shore occasionally.

- Makos are found all over the world in temperate and tropical waters.

- It is aggressive and very dangerous and is known to attack boats.

- The mako is highly prized by game fishermen.

BULL

- Part of the Carcharhiniforme group – the largest family of sharks.

- Scientific name: *Carcharinus leucas*.

- Also known as the Zambezi River or Lake Nicaragua shark.

- It grows up to 3.6 m (12 ft).

- It is grey on the dorsal side and white on the ventral side.

- Juveniles have dark-tipped fins and look very similar to black tip sharks.

- Bull sharks are found in the warmer waters of the world.

- They are also found in estuaries, and the freshwater areas of rivers and lakes.

- Bulls are very slow movers and conserve energy until food is located.

- They are known to be very aggressive and have often been implicated in attacks on humans.

TIGER

- Part of a group sometimes known as requiem sharks.

- It has the scientific name *Galeocerdo cuvier*.

- Tigers have curved, notched teeth, a short snout, and a sharply-pointed tail.

- They can grow up to 5.4 m (18 ft), but are usually 3.6-4.5 m (12-15 ft).

- The young have stripes on their sides and ventral surface, but these gradually diminish with age.

- Tigers live in tropical regions; offshore, inshore, and in estuaries.

- They are one of the most common sharks in the tropics.

- Tigers are second only to the great white in terms of the frequency of attacks on humans.

- It is a very aggressive shark that will eat just about anything.

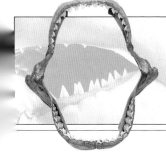

TIGER TEETH

Tiger sharks have multi-purpose teeth. The pointed tip impales prey, while the serrated bottom edges are for cutting. The teeth are extremely strong – tough enough to crunch through a turtle's bones and shell.

TIMES AND PLACES

- The waters between Sydney and Brisbane in Australia have a long history of shark attacks on humans.

- Amanzimtoti beach in South Africa is the most dangerous beach for shark attacks in the world.

- The islands of Hawaii have the greatest number of shark attacks in whole of the Pacific Ocean.

- The peak time of day for an attack is between 2 pm and 6 pm.

- Most shark attacks on humans occur during the summer months.

- Most shark attacks occur in less than 2 m (6 ft) of water.

- 25% of shark attacks occur within a short distance of the water's edge – just 10 m (30 ft) from the shore.

This map shows the areas where great white sharks have fatally attacked humans since 1876.

DANGER ZONES

- Inlets are often breeding grounds and so are thought of as a high-risk area.

- Channels where the water deepens suddenly are considered hazardous.

- Areas where garbage is dumped attracts sharks and should be avoided.

- Most attacks occur when the water is relatively calm.

- The waters around quays, docks, and wharfs should be avoided.

- Water clarity does not play a part in determining the likelihood of attack.

SWIMMING IN SHARK WATERS

- Never get out of your depth when swimming.

- Try not to swim on your own.

- Do not swim at night or at dusk.

- Never swim when bleeding, no matter how small the cut.

- Do not use the sea as a lavatory.

- Do not thrash about when swimming – erratic movement attracts sharks.

- Try not to make a lot of noise when in the sea.

HOW TO AVOID AN AGGRESSIVE SHARK

Advice for those who may come into contact with an aggressive shark…

- If a shark becomes aggressive, keep your eye on it.

- Try to move slowly and precisely.

- Keep your hands and arms close to your body.

- Get out of the water as quickly and calmly as possible.

- Inform other divers and swimmers to get out of the water.

- Tell a lifeguard or similar authority as soon as possible.

- It may seem obvious, but do not try to grab a shark!

Lifeguards scan the waters for sharks in high-risk areas.

SUITS

- A number of special suits have been developed to help protect divers from attack when studying sharks up close.

- Chain suits stop teeth from penetrating but do not stop crush injuries.

- Chain suits are very heavy and greatly decrease a diver's buoyancy and manoeuvrability.

- The "Neptunic" suit is a specially reinforced wet suit with chain mail over the top.

- A striped wet suit imitating a pilot fish or a sea snake has been tested.

- Unfortunately, the striped suit encouraged some sharks to attack.

CAGES

- Cages allow scientists and tourists to observe sharks at close range.

- Bait or chum is thrown into the water to attract the sharks.

- The cage is lowered into the water and floats on the surface. The occupants are never more than 3 m (9 ft) below the surface of the sea.

- When a feeding frenzy is observed, the only safe place is in a cage or out of the water completely.

- Shark cages are designed for observing larger sharks. Smaller sharks can get in through the gaps.

- On some occasions, sharks have surrounded a cage, making it impossible for the divers to get out safely.

CATCHING SHARKS

- Over 77,000 tonnes (75,768 tons) of sharks and rays are caught and killed each year.

- Dogfish is the most commonly fished shark for commercial reasons.

- Commercial fishing has little success as sharks breed very slowly, so stocks are wiped out quickly.

- Sport fishing for sharks is big business in many parts of the world. They are highly prized by game fishermen as trophies.

- To qualify for a record-breaking catch, the fisherman must have no help from anyone else until the fish is alongside the boat or shore.

TAKING THE BAIT

Studying sharks in an aquarium is the safest way to see them close up. Lemon sharks, such as the one in these photographs, cope well with living in captivity and are among the most commonly studied sharks.

The shark takes the bait...

...and shakes its head vigorously as it eats.

SHARK REPELLENTS

- The bang stick is an explosive device that detonates on contact with the shark. Its use is very dangerous.

- A shark screen is a water-filled plastic bag that holds a person upright in the water.

- The CO_2 dart gun fires a charge into the shark that expands in its body, giving it positive buoyancy and making it float to the surface.

- Gill nets have proved effective in protecting beaches. Sharks get caught in them and drown.

- Moses sole is a chemical placed on the skin that stops a shark from biting. It needs to be used in very large amounts to be effective.

- Experimental sonic devices have been used to shock, stun, and temporarily "blind" a shark.

SHARK INDUSTRY

SHARK SKINS

- Shark skin used commercially is sometimes called shagreen.

- Some shark skins are used like sandpaper to finish timber.

- Marble is polished to a high gloss using shark skins.

- The Japanese used shark skin on the handles of ceremonial swords.

- It was used in France to cover books, instrument cases, and scabbards.

- In the US, the Ocean Leather Company produces shoes, handbags, wallets, and belts from shark skin.

- Shark leather lasts twice as long as conventional leather.

FOOD

- Sharks fins are highly prized in Asia where they are used to make shark's fin soup.

- Shark is sometimes dyed and ground down for animal feed.

- Porbeagles and great whites are eaten in some parts of the world.

- Mako shark is often compared to tuna and is sometimes sold as sea sturgeon.

- Tope sharks are also caught off Australia and California.

- The Greenland shark is poisonous to eat.

- Many people won't eat shark because it is seen as distasteful.

SHARK SHACK

Sharks continue to fascinate people all over the world. The creature's menacing reputation and fearsome appearance has an attraction that is frequently exploited by companies for commercial purposes. The owner of this hot dog stand (right) has used the head of a shark in an attempt to attract customers to his business.

OTHER USES

- Shark jaws are sold to tourists and collectors. The jaws from a great white shark usually fetch the highest prices.

- Shark's teeth are used as ear-rings and necklaces.

- Sport fishermen will often have a shark stuffed and mounted on their wall.

- Extracts of a shark's gall bladder are believed to help acne sufferers and people with eye cataracts.

The blade of this knife has been made from hundreds of shark's teeth.

MEDICINE

- In 17th century France, shark brains were eaten in order to ease the pain of childbirth.

- Monsieur Pomet, the chief druggist to King Louis XIV of France, claimed that drinking white wine with shark's brain was excellent for gravel (kidney stones).

- Spiny dogfish oil has 10 times the amount of Vitamin A that cod liver oil contains.

- The levels of a chemical called squalene in liver oil may be the reason that sharks rarely get cancer.

- Shark oil also contains chemicals that can control cholesterol levels in human beings.

- Shark corneas have been used in transplant operations.

- A synthetic skin made from shark cartilage is sometimes used to treat burn victims.

- Shark oils are anticoagulants and have been used during heart surgery.

- Dried shark brain can be used to prevent tooth decay and as a general pain killer.

THE FUTURE FOR SHARKS

ENDANGERED SHARKS

- Up to 100 million sharks a year are killed by man.

- 1.8 million blue sharks are taken from the North Pacific each year.

- Game fishermen catch and release sharks, but the shark is so worn out from the fight that it usually dies shortly afterwards.

- The piked dogfish has declined in numbers as we take large numbers for food.

- Sharks are slow breeders and are unable to replace the caught fish.

- Sharks often get tangled in fishing nets and drown.

- After famous shark movies, many sharks were killed indiscriminately.

PROTECTION

- Marine reserves keep some sharks safe from man. Breeding grounds may need to be protected in the future.

- Fishing quotas could help save some species from extinction.

- Great whites are already protected in California, Australia, and South Africa.

- Basking sharks were fished almost to extinction, but they are now protected.

- International conventions, like the ones protecting whales, could be used.

- Some sharks have been kept in captivity to protect them from extinction.

- However, of the more than fifty types that have been kept in captivity, less than 10 species have survived for more than two months.

RESEARCH

- Shark tagging tells us a lot about shark numbers. Re-catching tagged sharks can also tell us about migration patterns.

- Radio tagging is a more advanced method of study. Sharks can be tracked electronically as they travel around the world.

- Most of our study revolves around grey reef sharks.

- Studying the physiology of the spiny dogfish may lead to a treatment for cystic fibrosis.

- We may be able to develop new antibiotics from shark liver.

TOURISM AND EDUCATION

- Sharks and rays are popular exhibits at marine aquaria.

- Walk-through tunnels allow people to see sharks up close.

- Shark dives are very popular with scuba divers.

- Underwater safaris educate people about the sea and its life.

- People on such underwater tours sign disclaimer forms, relieving the organizers of responsibility in the event of an attack.

- Feeding sharks while in the water has become a novelty in some parts of the Caribbean.

- People travel from all over the world to swim with sharks off the coast of the island of Borneo.

- Some great white sharks have become so used to humans that they eat from their hand.

- In South Africa, a few great white sharks enjoy having their snouts tickled by humans.

- "Shark tourism" has helped to improve the image of sharks, but could lead to problems.

- Some experts suggest that sharks that come into frequent contact with people could lose their natural fear of human beings.

- This could create the potentially dangerous situation of the sharks associating people with food, leading to an increase in attacks.

SHARK PARKS
This woman is holding her head inside the mouth of a model of great white shark at a sea life theme park in the US. The future of sharks as a part of our "entertainment" seems assured.

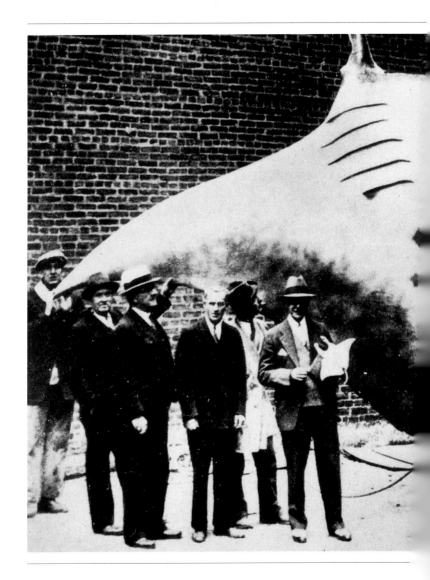

REFERENCE SECTION

SHARK TALES

SHARKS ARE AMAZING animals but difficult to study, so little is known about them. Many stories are told by sailors, islanders, and fishermen – anyone who encounters a shark usually has a tale to tell. The more we know and understand, the more we can learn to respect such misunderstood creatures.

RARE SPECIES

The megamouth was accidentally discovered in 1976, and only three specimens have since been recorded. Another four specimens have reportedly been found but have not been officially documented.

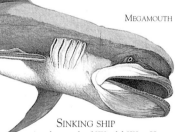

MEGAMOUTH

SINKING SHIP

At the end of World War II, *Indianapolis*, the ship that carried part of the Hiroshima atomic bomb was torpedoed by a Japanese submarine. Of the 883 people who died, most fell victim to sharks, which attacked the survivors for four days until help arrived.

DEADLY TAIL

A sailor is reported to have been decapitated by the tail of a thresher in the Atlantic. Fishermen must be particularly careful of the thresher's powerful tail as it is almost the same length as its body. The thresher shark is a prized catch. Its spectacular leaps out of the water make it a challenge to land on board.

BIZARRE SHARK

The goblin shark is one of the oddest-looking sharks. It was discovered off the coast of Japan, but was first known from fossil teeth about 100 million years old. The goblin or elfin shark is a deep-water species, coloured pink with a brownish tint.

GOBLIN SHARK

GREAT WHITE SHARK

PERSISTENT JAWS

In 1966, a very persistent great white bit the leg of a teenage boy at a surfing beach south of Sydney, Australia. The lifesavers who rescued the boy were stunned to realize that they would have to lift the body of the shark out of the water as well, as it refused to let go. It was not until the shark had been beaten over the head repeatedly that it opened its jaws. Amazingly, the boy's leg was saved.

GOURMET DELIGHT

The poisonous flesh of the greenland shark has a strong taste of ammonia, but is considered a delicacy in Iceland. The flesh is dried for several months before it is eaten. A strong, alcoholic local brew is served with the pieces of shark.

FOLLOW YOUR NOSE

Sharks have a remarkable sense of smell. Lemon sharks, under laboratory conditions, were found to be able to detect the scent of one part tuna fish to 25 million parts sea water. The hungrier the shark, the better its ability to detect the smell of fish in the water.

SLIM CHANCES

In Hawaii, the chance of drowning is more than 1,000 times greater than that of dying from a shark attack. In South Africa, the chance is 600 to 1, and in Australia, it is 50 to 1. However, bees kill more people in Australia each year than sharks do, while more people in the US are killed by lightning than by sharks.

SOLVING THE PUZZLE

In the 1980s, the US Navy was baffled by disc-shaped bites in the rubber coating of the listening devices on their submarines. By accident, a whale and shark expert was shown the bite marks, which he immediately identified as being those of the little cookiecutter shark.

ANCIENT SHARK

The frilled shark is much the same as sharks that lived 20 million years ago and is the most primitive living species. Its broad-based, pointed teeth are found only in fossil sharks.

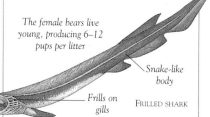

The female bears live young, producing 6–12 pups per litter

Snake-like body

Frills on gills

FRILLED SHARK

SHARK TALES 2

INCIDENTS INVOLVING sharks and humans occur every year; some are tragic, but others involve incredible escapes or unexplained shark activity. Sometimes, these events teach scientists more about these mysterious and fascinating sea creatures.

MAKO OR BREAK

In 1981, a 2-m (6-ft) Mako attacked 19-year-old Ted Best, a spearfisherman from Florida. The shark came close to Ted so he shot at it with his speargun. He pulled the spear out of the shark and tried to put it back in the gun for another shot. This was when the shark attacked him and bit his leg. The shark then let go and moved away. Best swam for shore and drove himself to a ranger's station, from where he was taken to hospital.

INCREASED THREAT

In 2000, shark attacks worldwide peaked at 79, the highest in four decades of researchers' records. Of these, 10 were fatal, including three in Australian waters after great white shark attacks. In 1999, 58 attacks were reported worldwide, and over the decade the number averaged 54 attacks a year. Experts believe the increasing number of attacks is due to more tourists taking holidays in places such as Florida and Australia to swim in the warm waters. Sharks may also be hunting closer to shore as a result of declining fish stocks.

UNUSUAL COMPANY

In August 2001, hundreds of sharks, some as long as 3 m (10 ft), congregated in the waters 4.8 km (3 miles) off Florida. Among the strange convergence were blacktips, bull sharks, hammerheads, and nurse sharks – species not normally seen moving together. Coastguards alerted swimmers and the sharks eventually moved out of the area.

Large number of ampullae of Lorenzini, which detect electric signals from hidden fish.

*HAMMER SCHOOLS
Hammerheads hunt as individuals at night but swim together in large numbers during the day.*

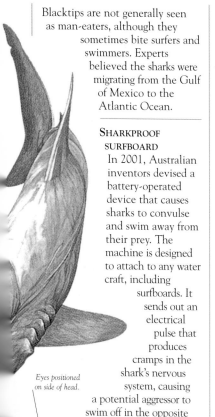

Blacktips are not generally seen as man-eaters, although they sometimes bite surfers and swimmers. Experts believed the sharks were migrating from the Gulf of Mexico to the Atlantic Ocean.

SHARKPROOF SURFBOARD

In 2001, Australian inventors devised a battery-operated device that causes sharks to convulse and swim away from their prey. The machine is designed to attach to any water craft, including surfboards. It sends out an electrical pulse that produces cramps in the shark's nervous system, causing a potential aggressor to swim off in the opposite

Eyes positioned on side of head.

SENSORY HEAD
Hammerheads' eyes are on the end of their head projections, giving them a good view as they swing their heads back and forth. The nostrils are widely spaced on the front of their heads, helping them detect where an odour is coming from.

direction. The inventors have tested it on the most feared of predators, the great white shark. The sharks scattered after receiving just a few strong pulses!

OFF THE MENU

In parts of Asia and elsewhere, shark fins are considered a delicacy. However, scientists have found evidence that they may contain dangerous amounts of the poison mercury – more than 40 times higher than the safe level for humans. The reason for this may be that the sharks have eaten fish contaminated by pollution in seawater. Up to 100 million sharks are killed each year by fishermen who slice off the fin and dump the creatures back into the sea. But only a handful of sharks attack humans each year, making dead sharks potentially more dangerous to human health than live ones.

EXTREME TOURISM

In 2001, when a dead whale floated into the waters off Adelaide, in Australia, it attracted the attention of great white sharks, which came to feed off its rotting body. However, it also attracted sightseers, who went out in boats to stand on the whale or touch the sharks, despite warnings from horrified local officials. Eventually, Australian police were forced to deal with the problem by detonating small explosives inside the whale to blow a hole in it and speed up its decomposition.

SHARK RECORDS

EVER SINCE HUMANS first ventured into the water, sharks have fascinated everyone who has encountered them. They come in many shapes and sizes and are indeed remarkable creatures. Scientists are still discovering new information about their biology and behaviour much of which is still unknown.

WHALE OF A FISH

The whale shark is the world's largest fish. The largest scientifically measured specimen was 12.65 m (41.5 ft) and weighed in at an estimated 15 to 21 tonnes (16.5 to 23 tons). It was caught off the coast of Pakistan in 1949. Lengths of over 18 m (59 ft) and weights of 40 tonnes (44 tons) have been reported.

BABY NUMBERS

The gestation period for sharks varies from nine to 22 months. The number of pups born at any one time ranges from one to 100.

OLDER THAN THE DINOSAURS

In terms of animal evolution, sharks are true survivors. They have probably changed less than any other type of vertebrate. One of the oldest fish fossil found so far is of a jawless, armoured fish called *Arandaspis*, discovered in central Australia. It has been dated to the Ordovician period, almost 500 million years ago.

SMALLEST SIZE

The spined pygmy shark is the world's smallest shark, measuring no more than 25 cm (10 in) long. It lives in deep, tropical waters. It has a spine on its first dorsal fin and is luminescent only on its underside, making it hard for predators swimming above to spot.

LONGEST DISTANCE

The blue is the greatest shark traveller. It has been tracked migrating distances of close to 6,000 km (3,726 miles) but mostly travels distances of about 2,500 km (1,553 miles). The mako, tiger, and sandbar sharks are all long-distance swimmers.

BLUE SHARK

FASTEST SWIMMERS

The blue shark and the mako shark are the fastest sharks. When catching food, the blue shark may accelerate to speeds of up to 69km/h (43 mph). It is not possible for sharks to sustain high speeds, and most rarely exceed 11 km/h (7 mph). The fastest fish in the sea is the sailfish which can reach 110 km/h (68 mph).

MOST ABUNDANT SHARK

The piked dogfish is one of the most common species found throughout the world. It is also the most widely eaten species and is fished in large numbers.

GREAT WHITE

MOST DANGEROUS

The great white is responsible for more attacks on humans than any other shark. Hammerheads and tiger sharks are also responsible for many attacks. The sharks that are a threat to people tend to be over 2 m (7 ft) in length. Because of its gruesome reputation, the great white has become endangered, with some countries now declaring it an officially protected species.

JAWS

Peter Benchley's novel *Jaws*, about a killer great white menacing residents of an American holiday resort, is one of the world's bestselling fiction titles. The first Hollywood movie based on the book, has become one of the top-grossing films of all time, spawning three sequels, including a 3-D version in which the shark seems to shoot right out of the screen.

SPINED PYGMY SHARK

This pygmy shark is actual size, and measures only 13 cm (5 in) long

SHARK ATTACK PREVENTION

ALTHOUGH THE RELATIVE risk of a shark attack is very small, attacks appear to be on the rise. In 2000, there were more attacks than in 40 years of records. However, risks can be minimized by heeding some general rules.

- Always stay in groups, since sharks are more likely to attack a person who is on their own.

- Do not wander too far from shore – this isolates an individual and additionally places one far away from any assistance that might be available.

- Avoid being in the water during darkness or twilight hours when most fish prey species are feeding, and sharks are likely to be active.

- Avoid swimming in areas where there are large schools of fish, or among seals or sea lions when they gather together in large groups.

- Do not enter the water if bleeding from an open wound or if menstruating – a shark's olfactory ability is acute.

- Do not wear shiny jewellery since the reflected light can resemble the sheen of fish scales.

- Sightings of porpoises do not indicate the absence of sharks – both often eat the same food items.

- Use extra caution when waters are murky and avoid uneven tanning and brightly coloured clothing – sharks see contrasts particularly well.

- Try not to splash too much and do not allow pets or domestic animals in the water because their erratic movements may attract schools of sharks.

• Be cautious when swimming between sandbars, near steep drop-offs, near channels, or at river mouths – sharks are often found here.

• Avoid swimming in areas where animal, human, or fish waste enters the water.

• Avoid swimming in areas where there are deep-water channels or drop-offs nearby.

• If you are spearing fish, do not carry dead or bleeding fish attached to you, and preferably remove all speared fish from the water as quickly as possible.

SEAL FROM BELOW   SURFER FROM BELOW

Sharks can often mistake the shape of a surfer for a seal, which is part of their natural diet.

• Do not enter the water if sharks are known to be present, and evacuate the water if sharks are seen while there.

• If you do see a large shark, leave the water as quickly and as calmly as possible. Remain out of the water until the shark has left the area.

AGGRESSIVE BODY LANGUAGE

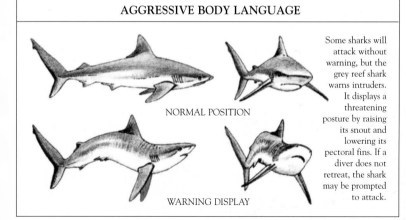

NORMAL POSITION

WARNING DISPLAY

Some sharks will attack without warning, but the grey reef shark warns intruders. It displays a threatening posture by raising its snout and lowering its pectoral fins. If a diver does not retreat, the shark may be prompted to attack.

SHARKS IN ART

WE MAY FEAR SHARKS and profess to hate them, but we are also thrilled by them. For centuries, we have told stories about them and drawn pictures of them. Sharks in literature are often adversaries, but ones that command respect, too. Sharks remind us of our essential powerlessness when faced with nature's impersonal violence.

THE OLD MAN AND THE SEA

In Ernest Hemingway's 1952 novel *The Old Man and the Sea*, an old man goes fishing off the coast of Cuba. There, he snares an impressive marlin fish, which immediately begins to attract other greedy predators. Over the course of one exhausting night, he battles with a gigantic mako shark, three shovel-nosed sharks, and then a further pack of sharks. The book is famed for its understanding of the ways of the sea, and for the equal respect Hemingway gives to humans and animals. However, Hemingway doesn't always stick rigorously to factual accuracy – he claims that the mako has eight rows of teeth when these fish have just two or three.

THE NARRATIVE OF A. GORDON PYM

Published in 1838, US writer Edgar Allen Poe's gothic sea novel *The Narrative of Arthur Gordon Pym* describes the shipwreck of a whaling vessel in the Atlantic Ocean. The sailors experience relentless horrors, including mutiny, savagery, cannibalism and frantic pursuits. They are surrounded for much of the time by huge

sharks. During one storm, the ship's deck slips under the water surface and a shark is thrown across deck, where its tail lashes one of the crew before the fish is swept back into the water. At another point, sharks eat the body of one of the sailors who died of hunger.

THE SHARK'S PARLOR

The US poet James Dickey's 1965 poem "The Shark's Parlor" describes an epic battle with a hammerhead shark, which is conducted from the front porch of a

seaside house. The house stands on wooden stilts and as the tide comes in and swirls beneath the floorboards, the narrator imagines fins circling beneath. Then he and a companion set bait and a fishing line, which attracts a real shark. Villagers are called to help reel the monster in, which is pulled right into the house in a fantastical dream-like scene.

DEEP BLUE SEA

In the 1999 movie *Deep Blue Sea*, researchers are trying to find the key to regenerating human brain tissue and, in the process, have been tinkering with the DNA codes of mako sharks at a floating research facility off the Mexican coast. This has the effect of making the sharks smarter and faster – and, as it turns out, much more dangerous. The sharks manage to escape from the holding tanks and turn on their tormentors. As the facility begins to sink, humans and sharks face one another on equal terms.

SHARK WORK

In 1997, the English artist Damien Hirst displayed an artwork composed of a glass tank in which a real tiger shark was preserved in green embalming fluid. Hirst called the work *The Physical Impossibility of Death in The Mind of Someone Living*. As the title implies, the shark looked terrifyingly alive – the viewer was confronted with its grinning mouth and beady eyes looking out from the green liquid.

SHARK MYTHS 1

DESPITE THEIR FEARSOME reputation and the way they are portrayed in movies and literature, the majority of sharks do not hurt people. Only 32 shark species have been documented in attacks on humans, and an additional 36 species are considered potentially dangerous. Despite this, many myths persist about these animals.

MOST SHARKS ARE HARMFUL TO PEOPLE
Untrue.
Of the more than 350 shark species, about 80% are unable to hurt people or rarely encounter humans.

SHARKS MUST ROLL ON THEIR SIDES TO BITE
No.
Sharks attack their prey in whichever way is most convenient, and they can protrude their jaws to bite prey in front of their snouts.

SHARKS EAT CONTINUOUSLY
Not true.
Sharks eat periodically, depending upon their metabolism and the availability of food. For example, young lemon sharks eat less than two percent of their body weight per day.

SHARKS PREFER HUMAN BLOOD
False.
Most sharks do not appear to be especially interested in the blood of mammals as opposed to fish blood.

Whale sharks are plankton-eaters and, although they are the largest species of shark, they pose no threat to humans.

SHARKS ARE NOT DISCRIMINATING EATERS AND SCAVENGE THE SEA
Wrong.
Most sharks prefer to eat certain types of invertebrates, fish and other animals. Some sharks eat mainly fish. Others eat other sharks or marine mammals. Some sharks are even plankton-eaters.

SHARKS ARE NOT FOUND IN FRESHWATER
Untrue.
A specialized osmoregulatory system enables the bull shark to cope with dramatic changes in salinity – from the freshwaters of some rivers to the highly saline waters of the ocean.

The bull shark lives in the warm waters of the world's oceans. It is one of the few sharks that spends time in freshwater, swimming far up rivers such as South America's Amazon and Africa's Zambezi.

WHALE SHARKS, THE LARGEST SPECIES OF SHARKS, ARE VORACIOUS PREDATORS
Incorrect.
Whale sharks, which are the largest fish that have ever lived, are plankton-feeders like the great whales, hence the name.

MOST SHARKS CRUISE AT HIGH SPEED WHEN THEY SWIM
Untrue.
Although some sharks may swim at bursts of over 20 knots (23 miles per hour), most sharks swim very slowly at cruising speeds of less than 5 knots (5.75 miles per hour).

SHARK MYTHS 2

MANY MYTHS ABOUT SHARKS arise as a result of our feelings of fear and fascination with these creatures. Often, the stories reported in newspapers and on television are exaggerated or untrue: every dark shadow in the waters seen by a swimmer cannot be a great white shark! Here are some more commonly held, but untrue, beliefs about sharks.

SHARKS HAVE POOR VISION
No.
Sharks' eyes, which are equipped to distinguish colours, employ a lens up to seven times as powerful as a human's. Some shark species can detect a light that is as much as 10 times dimmer than the dimmest light the average person can see.

EYES

Sharks can see well in dim light. Their eyes have a layer of cells called a tapetum that reflects light back onto the retina. In bright light they can close the pupil to a narrow slit. Some sharks even have a light-blocking screen to filter light.

Dogfish with closed pupil

Horn shark's pupil

Ray eye with screen

SHARKS HAVE PEANUT-SIZED BRAINS AND ARE INCAPABLE OF LEARNING
Inaccurate.
Sharks' relatively large and complex brains are comparable in size to those of supposedly more advanced animals like mammals and birds. Sharks can also be trained.

SHARK MEAT IS POISONOUS TO HUMANS
Wrong.
Although there have been some reports of people being poisoned by shark meat, the meat from the majority of sharks is edible when properly handled, prepared and cooked. In many countries, shark meat is often a luxury food in restaurants, providing a great source of protein.

THE GREAT WHITE SHARK IS A COMMON, ABUNDANT SPECIES FOUND OFF MOST BEACHES VISITED BY HUMANS
Not accurate.
Great whites are relatively uncommon large predators that prefer cooler waters. In some parts of their range, great whites are close to being endangered.

ALL SHARKS HAVE TO SWIM CONSTANTLY
Misconceived.
Some sharks can breathe by pumping water over their gills by opening and closing their mouths while at rest on the bottom.

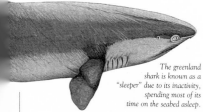

The greenland shark is known as a "sleeper" due to its inactivity, spending most of its time on the seabed asleep.

SHARKS ARE HARD TO KILL
Not true.
Stress of capture weakens a shark, and so some sharks are easily killed in hook-and-line or net fishing.

SHARKS ARE USELESS FISH
No way.
Sharks are a critical part of marine ecosystems, a source for knowledge to help medical conditions, and the basis of a valuable fishery.

SHARK ATTACKS IN PERSPECTIVE

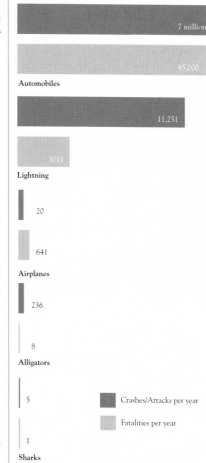

7 million

45,000

Automobiles

11,251

3011

Lightning

20

641

Airplanes

236

8

Alligators

5

1

Sharks

Crashes/Attacks per year

Fatalities per year

SHARK ATTACKS 2000

IN 2000, a total of 79 shark attacks were recorded, 10 of which were fatal. By comparison, 58 attacks were recorded in 1999, and the yearly average during the 1990s was 54.

NORTH AMERICA

The United States saw the majority of shark attacks in 2000, with a total of 50.

Alabama 2

Louisiana 1

North Carolina 5

South Carolina 1

Bahamas 4

Puerto Rico 1

California 3

Texas 2

Hawaii 2

Florida 34

PACIFIC OCEAN

Galapagos Islands 1

SOUTH AMERICA

ATLANTIC OCEAN

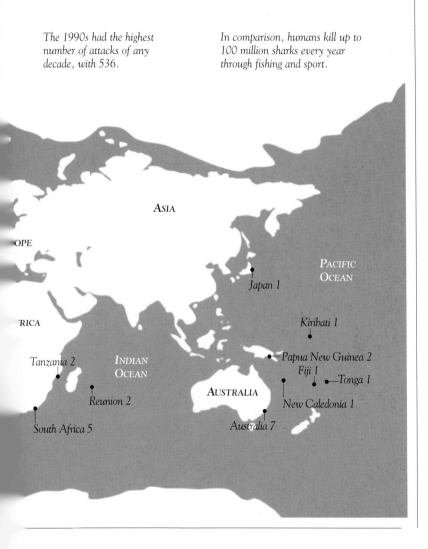

The 1990s had the highest number of attacks of any decade, with 536.

In comparison, humans kill up to 100 million sharks every year through fishing and sport.

ASIA

OPE

PACIFIC OCEAN

Japan 1

RICA

Kiribati 1

Tanzania 2

INDIAN OCEAN

Papua New Guinea 2

Fiji 1

Tonga 1

AUSTRALIA

Reunion 2

New Caledonia 1

South Africa 5

Australia 7

CLASSIFICATION

ANIMALS ARE CLASSIFIED into groups that share similar characteristics. Sharks are divided into eight orders. Each order contains families, which include genera and species. Only members of the same species can breed with one another.

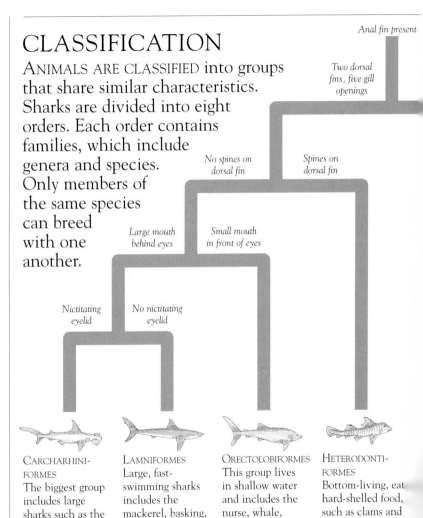

Anal fin present

Two dorsal fins, five gill openings

No spines on dorsal fin

Spines on dorsal fin

Large mouth behind eyes

Small mouth in front of eyes

Nictitating eyelid

No nictitating eyelid

CARCHARHINI-
FORMES
The biggest group includes large sharks such as the requiems and hammerheads.

LAMNIFORMES
Large, fast-swimming sharks includes the mackerel, basking, goblin, thresher, and mako sharks.

ORECTOLOBIFORMES
This group lives in shallow water and includes the nurse, whale, zebra, bamboo, and wobbegong sharks.

HETERODONTI-
FORMES
Bottom-living, eat hard-shelled food, such as clams and crabs: horn and Port Jackson shark

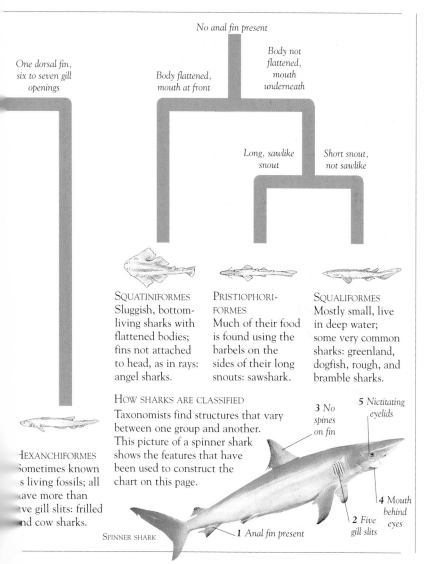

No anal fin present

One dorsal fin, six to seven gill openings

Body flattened, mouth at front

Body not flattened, mouth underneath

Long, sawlike snout

Short snout, not sawlike

SQUATINIFORMES
Sluggish, bottom-living sharks with flattened bodies; fins not attached to head, as in rays: angel sharks.

PRISTIOPHORI-FORMES
Much of their food is found using the barbels on the sides of their long snouts: sawshark.

SQUALIFORMES
Mostly small, live in deep water; some very common sharks: greenland, dogfish, rough, and bramble sharks.

HEXANCHIFORMES
Sometimes known as living fossils; all have more than five gill slits: frilled and cow sharks.

HOW SHARKS ARE CLASSIFIED
Taxonomists find structures that vary between one group and another. This picture of a spinner shark shows the features that have been used to construct the chart on this page.

3 No spines on fin

5 Nictitating eyelids

4 Mouth behind eyes

2 Five gill slits

1 Anal fin present

SPINNER SHARK

161

LAMNIFORMES

LAMNIFORMES, or mackerel sharks, make up seven families and 15 or 16 species. They are found worldwide, except in the coolest seas, ranging from inter-tidal regions to depths of more than 1,200 metres (4,000 feet), and from the surf line to the ocean basins.

MACKEREL SHARK

GREAT WHITE
A great white has over 100 functional teeth in its mouth, and many more waiting, when any break or become blunt.

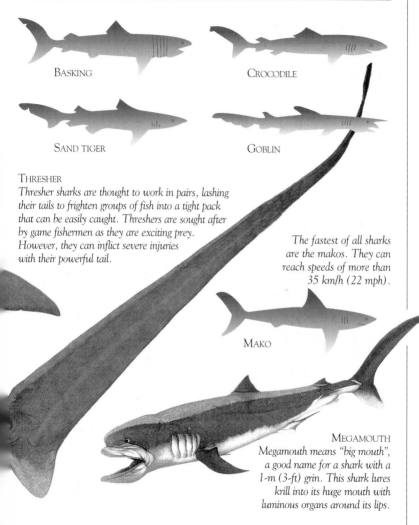

BASKING

CROCODILE

SAND TIGER

GOBLIN

THRESHER
Thresher sharks are thought to work in pairs, lashing their tails to frighten groups of fish into a tight pack that can be easily caught. Threshers are sought after by game fishermen as they are exciting prey. However, they can inflict severe injuries with their powerful tail.

The fastest of all sharks are the makos. They can reach speeds of more than 35 km/h (22 mph).

MAKO

MEGAMOUTH
Megamouth means "big mouth", a good name for a shark with a 1-m (3-ft) grin. This shark lures krill into its huge mouth with luminous organs around its lips.

163

CARCHARHINIFORMES

THE DOMINANT shark group around the world, carcharhiniformes make up eight families and 215 species. They are widespread, living in cold to tropical seas, as well as freshwater. Carcharhiniformes vary widely in size, but are generally uniform in shape – except for the hammerhead shark. This successful group of sharks has exploited a wide variety of habitats and food sources. Most of the potentially dangerous sharks occur in this group.

REQUIEM

BULL

TIGER
The tiger shark eats anything from sea lions to crabs. It is the most feared shark after the great white. Its teeth can carve large chunks out of prey.

HAMMERHEAD

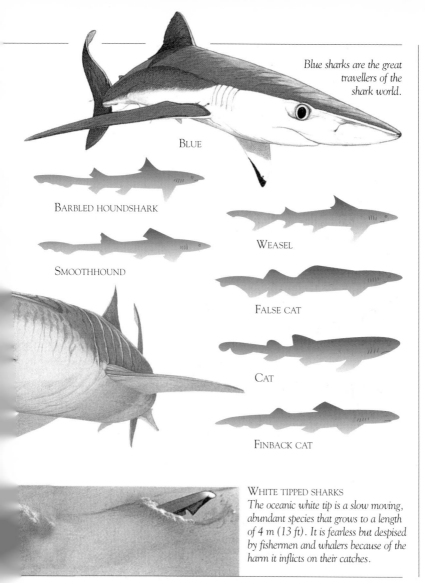

Blue sharks are the great travellers of the shark world.

BLUE

BARBLED HOUNDSHARK

SMOOTHHOUND

WEASEL

FALSE CAT

CAT

FINBACK CAT

WHITE TIPPED SHARKS
The oceanic white tip is a slow moving, abundant species that grows to a length of 4 m (13 ft). It is fearless but despised by fishermen and whalers because of the harm it inflicts on their catches.

165

ORECTOLOBIFORMES

ORECTOLOBIFORMES, or ground sharks, make up seven families and 37 species of shark. They are found in warmer temperate or tropical waters in shallow to moderate depths – largely the tropics of the western Pacific and Indian oceans. They vary in size, colour and markings.

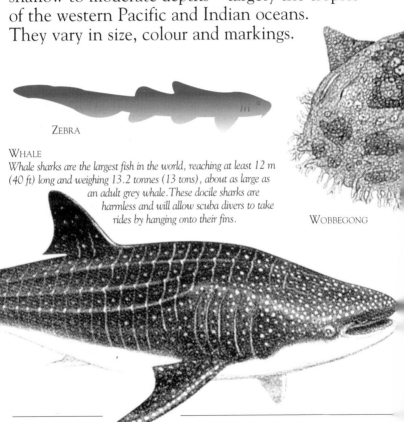

ZEBRA

WHALE
Whale sharks are the largest fish in the world, reaching at least 12 m (40 ft) long and weighing 13.2 tonnes (13 tons), about as large as an adult grey whale. These docile sharks are harmless and will allow scuba divers to take rides by hanging onto their fins.

WOBBEGONG

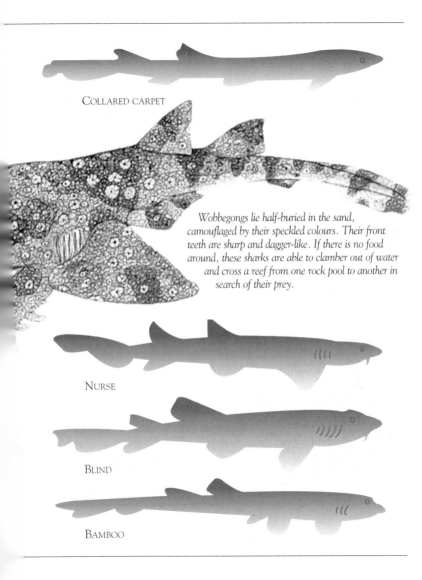

COLLARED CARPET

Wobbegongs lie half-buried in the sand, camouflaged by their speckled colours. Their front teeth are sharp and dagger-like. If there is no food around, these sharks are able to clamber out of water and cross a reef from one rock pool to another in search of their prey.

NURSE

BLIND

BAMBOO

HETERODONTIFORMES

THIS GROUP, also known as bullhead sharks, is made up of just eight members, all of which are very similar in shape. They are all bottom dwellers that feed on crustaceans and most also have a poisonous spine before each dorsal fin. Bullhead sharks are a harmless group and never grow very large, making them popular in aquariums.

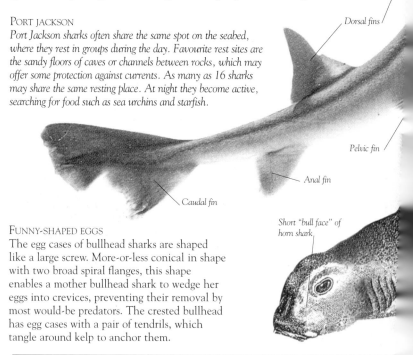

PORT JACKSON

Port Jackson sharks often share the same spot on the seabed, where they rest in groups during the day. Favourite rest sites are the sandy floors of caves or channels between rocks, which may offer some protection against currents. As many as 16 sharks may share the same resting place. At night they become active, searching for food such as sea urchins and starfish.

Dorsal fins

Pelvic fin

Anal fin

Caudal fin

Short "bull face" of horn shark

FUNNY-SHAPED EGGS

The egg cases of bullhead sharks are shaped like a large screw. More-or-less conical in shape with two broad spiral flanges, this shape enables a mother bullhead shark to wedge her eggs into crevices, preventing their removal by most would-be predators. The crested bullhead has egg cases with a pair of tendrils, which tangle around kelp to anchor them.

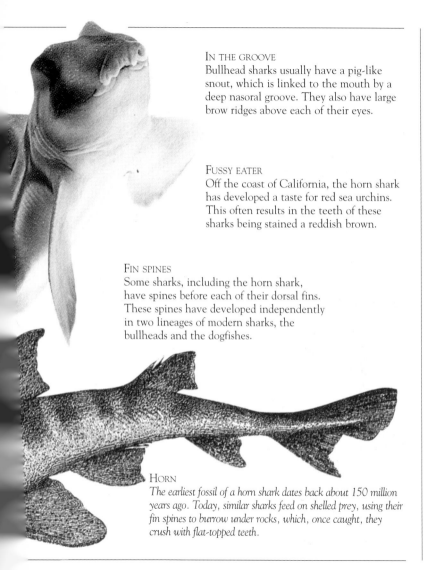

IN THE GROOVE
Bullhead sharks usually have a pig-like snout, which is linked to the mouth by a deep nasoral groove. They also have large brow ridges above each of their eyes.

FUSSY EATER
Off the coast of California, the horn shark has developed a taste for red sea urchins. This often results in the teeth of these sharks being stained a reddish brown.

FIN SPINES
Some sharks, including the horn shark, have spines before each of their dorsal fins. These spines have developed independently in two lineages of modern sharks, the bullheads and the dogfishes.

HORN
The earliest fossil of a horn shark dates back about 150 million years ago. Today, similar sharks feed on shelled prey, using their fin spines to burrow under rocks, which, once caught, they crush with flat-topped teeth.

HEXANCHIFORMES

ALSO KNOWN as frilled and cow sharks, hexanchiformes are the most ancient order. The most distinguishable feature is the possession of six or even seven gill slits – a primitive feature, since most modern sharks possess only five gill slits. Compared to sharks of other orders, frilled and cow sharks only have one dorsal fin. They are found worldwide, living mostly in deeper waters. Our knowledge about their biology is still fragmentary.

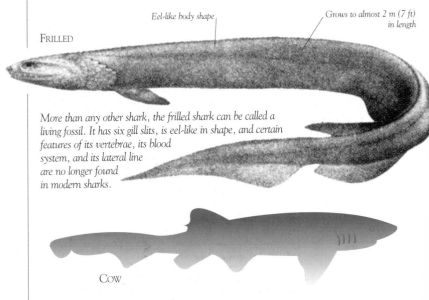

FRILLED

Eel-like body shape

Grows to almost 2 m (7 ft) in length

More than any other shark, the frilled shark can be called a living fossil. It has six gill slits, is eel-like in shape, and certain features of its vertebrae, its blood system, and its lateral line are no longer found in modern sharks.

COW

SQUATINIFORMES

FLATTENED, ALMOST ray-like sharks which live on the seabed. They have small, sharp teeth for catching and holding fish prey. There are 12 species, and they live in depths from shallow waters to 1,300 metres (4,300 feet).

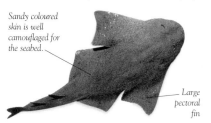

Sandy coloured skin is well camouflaged for the seabed.

Large pectoral fin

ANGEL
There are 13 different kinds of angel shark and all live in shallow, warm seas, though some migrate to warmer waters during the summer. They hunt at night in their own territories. Unlike rays, they have sharp teeth for feeding on shelled prey and small fish.

PRISTIOPHORIFORMES

ALSO KNOWN as saw sharks. Characterized by a long, slender, saw-like snout equipped with sharp, tooth-like projections on each edge. A very unusual group that is often confused with sawfishes, which are rays. The most obvious difference between the two is that saw sharks possess barbels, and the teeth, located on the prolonged snout, are different sizes. Only five species are known. Saw sharks are found off South Africa, Australia, and eastern Asia. Not much is known about the general biology of this order.

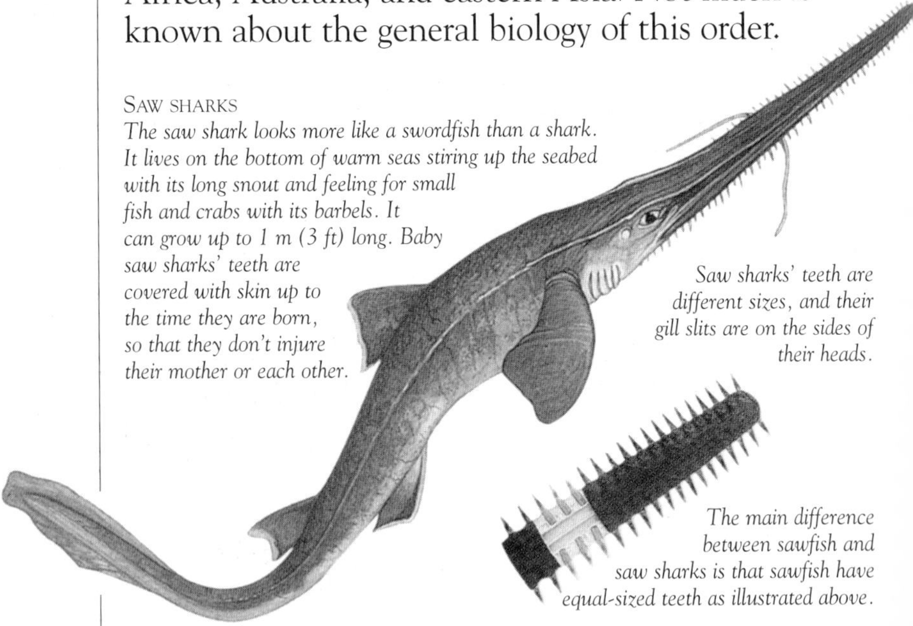

SAW SHARKS
The saw shark looks more like a swordfish than a shark. It lives on the bottom of warm seas stiring up the seabed with its long snout and feeling for small fish and crabs with its barbels. It can grow up to 1 m (3 ft) long. Baby saw sharks' teeth are covered with skin up to the time they are born, so that they don't injure their mother or each other.

Saw sharks' teeth are different sizes, and their gill slits are on the sides of their heads.

The main difference between sawfish and saw sharks is that sawfish have equal-sized teeth as illustrated above.

SQUALIFORMES

DEEPWATER SHARKS found worldwide in a range of environments, both inshore and offshore, in the tropics and in cold seas. The largest of the group, the Greenland shark, is restricted to boreal, Arctic, and sub-Antarctic waters where it even occurs in the most unlikely place to find a shark – beneath ice-floes. Some, such as the gulper sharks, inhabit depths well over 1,000 metres (3,300 feet), while others such as the spiny dogfish *Squalus acanthias* prefer the shallower environment of shelf and coastal waters, even entering the intertidal regions. Much is still uncertain about this large and diverse group of sharks.

There is evidence that gulper sharks make vertical migrations to the middle depths of the ocean where more food is available.

The Greenland shark is known to be a deep water "sleeper".

GULPER

GREENLAND

BRAMBLE

DOGFISH

SKATES AND RAYS

SKATES AND RAYS ARE FOUND IN NEARLY all the oceans of the world, from shallow areas to depths of more than 2,700 metres (8,900 feet). Between 300 and 350 species of skates and rays are known to exist. They vary in size from a few centimetres in length to the giant mantas that may grow to about 7 metres (23 feet) wide and weigh more than 1,360 kilograms (3,000 pounds).

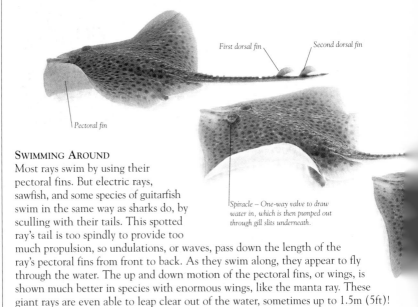

First dorsal fin

Second dorsal fin

Pectoral fin

SWIMMING AROUND

Most rays swim by using their pectoral fins. But electric rays, sawfish, and some species of guitarfish swim in the same way as sharks do, by sculling with their tails. This spotted ray's tail is too spindly to provide too

Spiracle – One-way valve to draw water in, which is then pumped out through gill slits underneath.

much propulsion, so undulations, or waves, pass down the length of the ray's pectoral fins from front to back. As they swim along, they appear to fly through the water. The up and down motion of the pectoral fins, or wings, is shown much better in species with enormous wings, like the manta ray. These giant rays are even able to leap clear out of the water, sometimes up to 1.5m (5ft)!

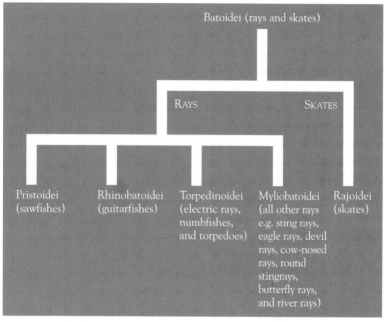

Batoidei (rays and skates)

Rays

Skates

Pristoidei (sawfishes)

Rhinobatoidei (guitarfishes)

Torpedinoidei (electric rays, numbfishes, and torpedoes)

Myliobatoidei (all other rays e.g. sting rays, eagle rays, devil rays, cow-nosed rays, round stingrays, butterfly rays, and river rays)

Rajoidei (skates)

POISON GLAND
Some rays have sharp, saw-like stingers on their tails. These are good protection against their enemies.

SKATES AND RAYS: FACTS

SKATES AND RAYS ARE odd-looking creatures, with their eyes on one side of their flat bodies and their mouths on the other. When not lying on the seabed waiting for prey to pass overhead, they swim like birds, flapping their wing-like pectoral fins to propel themselves through the water. In some parts of the world, where they are known to congregate around a food source, skates and rays have become popular tourist attractions.

STING IN THE TAIL

The largest stingrays are powerful enough to lash their tails through the hull of a wooden boat. The spines on the tails cause serious and extremely painful wounds that can kill.

FISHING FOR A CURE

In the early 20th century, stingrays were extensively fished. They were caught for their liver oil, which is thought to be a cure for ailments such as rheumatism. Fishermen even soaked their underwear in the oil to protect themselves from bitter weather!

MANTA RAY ACROBATICS

Scientists have observed manta rays and eagle rays jumping out of the water, seemingly for fun! Three types of jumps have been observed: jumping forwards and landing head-first, jumping forwards and landing tail-first, and backward somersaults.

TAGGING RAYS

Although scientists know that manta rays are migratory animals, the details of these seasonal journeys are not known. Projects are underway to tag the rays with coloured strips, so that their movements can be observed.

MISTAKEN THREAT

Although manta rays are one of the world's most gentle sea creatures, they were once thought to be capable of destroying fishing boats and the fishermen inside them. Sailors called them devil fish, after the large "horns" that extended forward from their heads. In fact, these horns are ingenuous scoopers which, when unfurled, guide plankton into the manta's mouth.

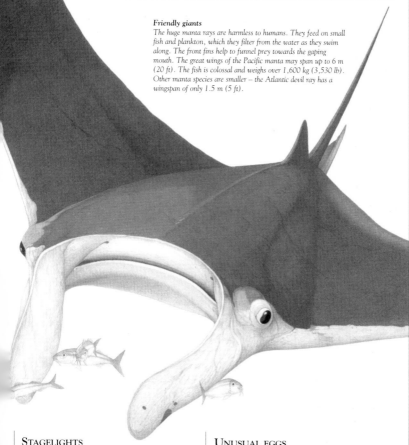

Friendly giants
The huge manta rays are harmless to humans. They feed on small fish and plankton, which they filter from the water as they swim along. The front fins help to funnel prey towards the gaping mouth. The great wings of the Pacific manta may span up to 6 m (20 ft). The fish is colossal and weighs over 1,600 kg (3,530 lb). Other manta species are smaller – the Atlantic devil ray has a wingspan of only 1.5 m (5 ft).

STAGELIGHTS

On Hawaii's Kona Coast, mantas are drawn each evening to the lights of a large hotel. Night divers watch as the mantas feed on the plankton that is also attracted by the lights.

UNUSUAL EGGS

Unlike rays, which bear live young, skates lay flattened, rectangular eggs with tendrils at the corners. Empty egg cases are often found on beaches and are known as mermaids' purses.

Resources

PLACES WHERE YOU CAN SEE SHARKS

The best place to view sharks in the wild is the tropics. Alternatively, most aquariums have shark exhibits, and some allow visitors to touch sharks and rays. Here is a list of some aquariums, most of which have conservation programmes as well as viewing tanks or larger displays.

AUSTRALIA
Sydney Aquarium at Darling Harbour
Pier 26
Darling Harbour
Sydney NSW 2000

Oceanworld Manly
West Esplanade
Manly NSW 2095

Great Barrier Reef Aquarium
East Flinders Street
Townsville QLD 4810

Perth Underwater World
Hillarys Boat Harbour
Hillarys WA 6025

UNITED KINGDOM
Blackpool Aquarium
12 Clifton Street
Blackpool
Lancashire FY1 1JP

Poole Aquarium
Hennings Wharf
The Quay
Poole, Dorset PH15 1HJ

London Aquarium
County Hall, Riverside Building
Westminster Bridge Road
London SE1 7PB

United states
Aquarium for Wildlife Conservation
Surf Avenue and West 8th Street, Brooklyn, New York 11224

National Aquarium in Baltimore
Pier 3, 501 East Pratt Street
Baltimore, Maryland 21202

Seattle Aquarium
1483 Alaskan Way
Seattle, Washington 98101

Sea World
1720 South Shores Road
San Diego, California 92109

Sea World
7007 Sea World Drive
Orlando, Florida 32821

ORGANIZATIONS INTERESTED IN SHARKS

UNITED KINGDOM
Basking Shark Protection Group
Cronk Mooar
Curragh Road
St Johns, Isle of Man
AM4 8LN

Mr Rolf Williams
28 Fursby Avenue
West Finchley
London N3 1PL
Club that caters especially for children and schools.

European Elasmobranch Association
36 Kingfisher Court
Hambridge Road
Newbury
Berkshire RG14 5SJ

Traffic
219 Huntington Road
Cambridge CB3 0DL
Wildlife monitoring and
other conservation
activities.

Shark Research Bureau
60 Park House, Bridge
Row, Welwyn Garden
City, Hertfordshire
AL8 6TP

**National Federation of
Sea Anglers**
Mr J. F Reece
Pamplona
11 Downs Road
Hastings
Sussex TN34 2DX

**Marine Conservation
Society**
Dr Rober Earli
9 Gloucester Road
Ross-on-Wye
Herdfordshire HR9 5BU

**Sea Life Centre
(Blackpool) Ltd**
Blackpool
Lancashire FY1 5AA

UNITED STATES
**International Union for
the Conservation of
Nature (ICUN)**
Bimini Biological Field
Station
University of Miami
9300 Southwest 99th
Street
Miami Florida 33176
Ten regional Shark
Specialist Groups
responsible to the IUCN
cover all tropical seas.

**Pelagic Shark Research
Foundation**
333 Lake Avenue
Santa Cruz Yacht Harbour
Santa Cruz, California
95060

SOME SHARK
PUBLICATIONS

Life of Sharks
P. Brudker, Columbia
University Press, 1971

Shark Attack
Victor Coppleston, first
published 1958, revised
edition 1976 (Australia)

The Book of Sharks
Richard Ellis, Rober Hall
(London), 1983

*Natural History of
Sharks*
T.H Linneaweaver III and
R Backus, Andre Deutsch,
1970

Eyewitness Shark
Miranda Macquitty,
Dorling Kindersley, 1992

Sharks and Survival
edited by W.G Perry, D.C
Heath and Co, Boston

Sharks in Question
A Smithsonian Answer
Book, Victor G. Springer
and Joy P. Gold, 1989

Sharks
Rodney Steele, Blandford
Press, 1985

*Sharks, Silent Hunters
of the Deep*
Introduction by R and V
Taylor, published by
Reader's Digest, 2nd
revision, 1994

179

GLOSSARY

Adaptation
An evolutionary process that enables living things to fit their environment as perfectly as possible.

Ampullae of Lorenzini
Pores around the snout and head of a shark that contain organs sensitive to weak electric charges in the water.

Ampullae of Lorenzini

Anal fin
A small fin on the underside of a shark located near its tail.

Barbel
A sensitive, finger-like projection near the mouth of some sharks and other fish that enables them to detect food hidden in mud or sand.

Cartilaginous fish
Fish that have skeletons formed of cartilage, not bone. They include sharks, skates, rays, chimeras, and banjo fish.

Caudal fin
The tail fin.

Cartilage
A firm, gristly material that forms the skeletons of sharks. It is not as hard as bone, though it may be strengthened by calcium salts.

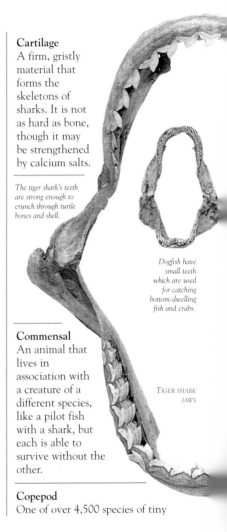

The tiger shark's teeth are strong enough to crunch through turtle bones and shell.

Dogfish have small teeth which are used for catching bottom-dwelling fish and crabs.

TIGER SHARK JAWS

Commensal
An animal that lives in association with a creature of a different species, like a pilot fish with a shark, but each is able to survive without the other.

Copepod
One of over 4,500 species of tiny

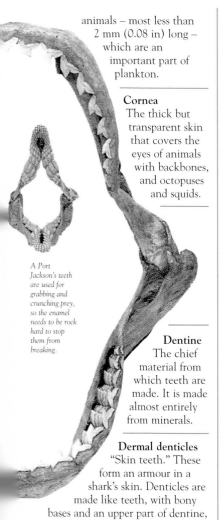

animals – most less than 2 mm (0.08 in) long – which are an important part of plankton.

Cornea
The thick but transparent skin that covers the eyes of animals with backbones, and octopuses and squids.

A Port Jackson's teeth are used for grabbing and crunching prey, so the enamel needs to be rock hard to stop them from breaking.

Dentine
The chief material from which teeth are made. It is made almost entirely from minerals.

Dermal denticles
"Skin teeth." These form an armour in a shark's skin. Denticles are made like teeth, with bony bases and an upper part of dentine, covered with enamel. Most dermal denticles have minute ridges, which help to guide water over a shark's side so that it swims more efficiently.

Dorsal fin
A fin on the mid-line of the back of a fish.

Dorsal fin on brownbanded shark

Dorsal fin on epaulette shark

Ecologist
A person involved in the study of the environment.

Enamel
The hard covering to the exposed part of a tooth. It is the hardest part of an animal's body.

Embryo
A developing animal before it is born or hatched from an egg.

Feeding frenzy
The way that sharks compete for food, regardless of their own safety, when there is blood or abundant food in the water.

Fossil
A plant or animal that lived long ago but became preserved in rock after it died.

Spiral fossil teeth

Gall bladder
A small pouch attached to the liver, which stores a substance called bile. Bile has various functions, the most important of which is aiding the digestion of fat.

Gestation
The period that an embryo takes to develop before birth.

Gill raker
A comb-like organ growing from a gill arch of a fish, including some sharks. Its function is to strain tiny organisms from the water as it passes over the fish's gills.

Gills
The breathing organs of fish through which oxygen is taken into the animal's body and waste carbon dioxide is expelled into the water.

Gill slits

In sharks and their relatives, the gills are unprotected and can be seen as a series of between five and seven slits just behind the head.

Interneurals
Part of the structure of a vertebra of a shark.

Lateral line
A series of pressure-sensitive organs around the head and forming a line down the side of a fish.

Indication of lateral line on a catshark.

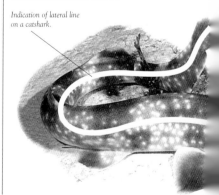

The frilled shark has five gill openings.

Migration
Regular movement of an animal population from one area to another and back again, usually on a yearly basis.

Nictitating membrane
Often called the third eyelid, the nictitating membrane moves across the surface of the eye to clean and protect it.

Olfactory
Concerning the sense of smell.

Ovoviviparous
Reproduction where the young develop inside the body, but when born, lack a placenta and rely on a yolk sac.

Shagreen
The dried skin of a shark. At one time, used like sandpaper for polishing marble and other hard substances.

Tapetum
A layer of cells that lies behind the retina of some fish and nocturnal animals. It reflects light back into the eye, so that it is used most effectively in dim conditions.

Vertical migration
Movement of marine creatures from one level in the water to another. Many planktonic organisms make vertical migrations daily. They may be followed by fish and other predators.

Plankton is largely made up of tiny marine plants and animals that float at the mercy of the currents.

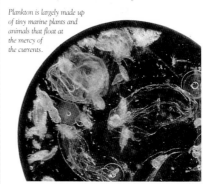

Viviparous
Reproduction where the young stay in the mother's body until they are ready to be born.

Latin name index

Index